ONE IN A SERIES FROM THE PUBLISHERS OF *PRE-K TODAY*

LEARNING THROUGH PLAY

SCIENCE

A Practical Guide for Teaching Young Children

Written by Susan Bromberg Kleinsinger

▪

Foreword by Barbara Sprung

Contributing Writers:

Ellen Booth Church

Lisa Feeney

Scott Hewit, Ed.D.

Merle Karnes, Ed.D.

Karen Miller

Kathy Spitzley

Connie Ward

Illustrated by Nicole Rubel

Early Childhood Division Vice President and Publisher
Helen Benham

Art Director
Sharon Singer

Art Editor
Toby Fox

Production Editor
Katie Lyons

Editors
Nancy-Jo Hereford
Jane Schall

Copyright © 1991 by Scholastic Inc.

Published by:
Scholastic Inc.
Early Childhood Division
730 Broadway
New York, NY 10003

ISBN # 0-590-49114-8
Library of Congress Catalog Number

CONTENTS

LEARNING AND GROWING WITH SCIENCE

Your Role in Fostering Science Discovery.............................7
  ▪ Ages and Stages...7
  ▪ Science With Mixed Age Groups.................................12

Exploring Science:
Hands-on Themes for Young Scientists.............................14
  ▪ Field-Trip Tips...19

Learning and Growing Through Science:
Developmental Chart...22

Exploring Science With Special-Needs Children...................26

Setting Up for Science..28

Sharing the Wonder of Science With Families.....................33

Discovering Science Together at Home............................34

ACTIVITY PLANS FOR TWOS, THREES, FOURS, AND FIVES

Using the Activity Plans..36
TWOS..38
THREES..48
FOURS...58
FIVES...68

Activity Plan Index...78

Resources...80

Cover Photo: James Levin

FOREWORD
A Conversation With Barbara Sprung
Helping Every Child Feel at Home in Your Science Center

Barbara Sprung founded the Non-Sexist Child Development Project at the Women's Action Alliance in 1972 and created the first non-sexist curriculum for early childhood educators. In 1982, she co-founded Educational Equity Concepts, where she continues to develop materials free of sex, race, and disability bias.

Q: As co-author of a non-sexist science curriculum for young children, why do you feel science is a particular concern?

A: From preschool to college, we don't do enough to encourage girls and children of color to engage in science. A dozen years ago, only 5 percent of our scientists were women and only 1.5 percent were black, and those figures have not greatly improved. Research tells us that 80 percent of jobs in the future will require knowledge of science and math. But we have not put that into our psyche at the early childhood level. We have to broaden our outlook. Science needs to have as important a focus in the early childhood curriculum as does language and social development.

Q: Why is it important that every young child engage in science activities on a regular basis?

A: Early childhood teachers have the incredibly important job of laying the foundation for all future learning. If we leave out the science block — or don't emphasize it equally for everyone — then starting in preschool, a huge sphere of learning may be closed off to many children. How can our nation survive if we don't develop every member of our future work force to his or her fullest capacity? We would never knowingly limit options and opportunities in other ways, yet too often we say of science, "Oh, that can come later." We must stop thinking that way. We must give science the same emphasis we give teaching children to listen, to love literature, and to speak in whole sentences.

Q: Could you offer some practical suggestions?

A: Yes. I think we have to look at our day broadly and consider how many whole-group "required" activities are language-oriented — the area where boys most often need help. We must do the same to encourage girls to develop visual/spatial and problem-solving skills, the areas where they aren't always strong: These skills are needed to excel in science and engineering, in mathematics and computers. We must ensure that every child develops all the vital skills, that every child experiences literature and science and block building.

Q: Should a teacher actively intervene if some children shy away from science and the science center?

A: I was trained as an early childhood teacher to believe that you create a rich environment, then let children select what they want to do. I've come a long way from that view. Research shows that children at an early age display sex-defined preferences and skills. In light of that, I believe intervention is necessary, but I also feel that it must be carried out in non-obtrusive, non-threatening ways. I think a teacher can say to children, "Everything in this room is here for a special reason. Sometimes you'll choose what you want to do, and sometimes we'll do new things together."

The teacher is a role model and an advocate. If a teacher — let's say a woman — sits in the science center or in the block corner and demonstrates strong interest in these areas, or even says to the group that she would like everyone to experiment today or build today — and does that on a regular basis — every child's interest in these areas will be enhanced.

I once observed a teacher whose three-year-olds were working with water and sieves. One little girl was very reluctant to join in. The teacher put her arm around the child and said, "I want you to try this." The teacher wasn't coercive. She didn't say, "You have to do this." She said, "I'll be there, come along with me." Well, once the child started playing, she didn't want to stop. But she would never have selected that activity without encouragement.

Q: Do early childhood teachers realize how much potential they have to set non-sexist attitudes in young children?

A: I think we do intuitively, but I'm not sure it's talked about enough. For me, one of the most gratifying aspects of working with young children is watching change occur. If you're focusing on an area such as science, from a year's beginning to end, you can see enormous changes in children's attitudes about who belongs in the science center.

Our programs work to empower teachers and parents to recognize that they know more science than they think they do, that science is not something "out there," only for experts, but the stuff of everyday life. We must impart that understanding to children, not by telling them but by giving them the means to make those discoveries on their own.

I was still teaching in a preschool when I first started focusing on equity issues. Parents whose older children I had also taught kept saying to me, "What's different this year?" After some serious reflection, I realized my *attitude* was different. I was treating boys and girls more equally. We've all been socialized in the same system, and much of what we do to reinforce sex-role stereotypes is unconscious. But a little awareness can go a long way.

Q: How far have we come in the past 20 years to free children from stereotyped sex roles and attitudes?

A: Not far enough. There was progress throughout the '70s, but we lost ground in the '80s. You can see it in children's clothes and toys. The message now is that you can't pass on a blue bicycle to a little girl: Hers should be lavender and pink. We need to redouble our efforts, and we must "begin at the beginning." Teachers of young children are in a strong position to change attitudes.

Barbara Sprung is a pioneer in the development of early childhood programs and materials that are non-sexist, multicultural, and provide positive images of children and adults with disabilities. Along with Merle Froschl and Patricia Campbell, she wrote What Will Happen If ..., *a non-sexist science curriculum for young children, published by Educational Equity Concepts. A tireless advocate of bias-free education, Sprung recently formed the Sex-Equity Caucus, which meets yearly at the annual conference of the National Association for the Education of Young Children.*

The important thing is not to stop questioning.
Albert Einstein

YOUR ROLE
IN FOSTERING
SCIENCE DISCOVERY

Photo: James Levin

Children are natural scientists, born with a sense of wonder and a passionate drive to find out about their world. As an important adult in their lives, you play a critical role in helping young children to experience that sense of wonder and discovery. In doing so, they begin to understand the world around them. Your acceptance, encouragement, and support of their boundless curiosity will help to keep the scientist alive in every child.

DO YOU NEED TO BE A SCIENCE EXPERT?

Let's be clear about one thing from the start — you do *not* need to be a science expert to help young children experience and enjoy successful science activities. What you do need to know is your children — what they're curious about, what they like to do, what holds their interest, and how they learn best. Then you need to use what you know about them to look for ways to build in science experiences that draw on their interests, letting children make decisions for themselves as they explore, discover, and learn.

You also need to be a resource for children. Again, that doesn't mean you have to know all the answers. In fact, it's much more meaningful and exciting when you ask children what they think, rather than telling them what they should know. If they come up with

AGES & STAGES
IN THE SCIENCE CENTER

How children approach science activities depends on their experiences, ages, and developmental levels. Use these guidelines as you plan and observe.

Two-year-olds:
- learn best through direct activities, supplemented by materials labeled with simple, realistic pictures. Movement activities, songs, and fingerplays related to science experiences aid learning.
- show interest in many things but have a short attention span for each. Open-ended activities that involve physical activity or sensory exploration, like water, sand, or magnet play, are most likely to hold children's interest.
- prefer activities that are self-directed and allow for choice. Children often use materials in unexpected ways.
- enjoy repeating activities over and over; for example, filling a container with water, then dumping it out and starting again.
- play parallel to others, observing and imitating but usually not interacting directly.
- have difficulty sharing space and materials. They may grab from others and hoard items.
- understand more than they can

say, relying highly on gestures to relate their experiences.
■ need adults nearby to define boundaries, set behavioral limits, and help solve conflicts.

Three-year-olds:

■ begin to explore and experiment with greater intent and direct their efforts toward an outcome.
■ prefer physical activities and sensory exploration. However, they are able to take in information that directly relates to an experience through conversation and books with simple text.
■ enjoy adult-directed science experiences for short periods, but are most productive when activities are self-selected and directed.
■ ask questions about everything but don't always understand the answers. They begin to recognize cause-and-effect relationships as they ask why and how.
■ have rapidly developing language skills. They relate and discuss events, but may have difficulty pronouncing words and putting their thoughts in order, especially when stressed or excited. They need adults to listen carefully and "translate" what they say.
■ learn most easily within the context of personally meaningful activities and a trusting bond with teachers and caregivers.

Four-year-olds:

■ are taking in enormous amounts of information about their world. They use pretend

"wrong" answers, plan experiences that will guide them to find out for themselves. Or better yet, find out together.

You are a special role model. Children will be motivated by your curiosity and desire to find out. On a personal side, to encourage children to make science discoveries, you need the very qualities that children possess in abundance — an urge to question, to explore, and to experiment. As you know, the excitement of discovery is contagious. Your own positive attitude and approach to science experiences will give your children a strong start for all later learning.

WHAT IS SCIENCE?

While knowing a lot of scientific facts and theories may not be necessary, it is important to understand the fundamentals of science and to know how science experiences benefit children. This is especially valuable when discussing the aims of your science program with families. This refresher may help.

■ *What is science?* Science, as a subject, refers to a field of study that includes facts and theories which help to describe and explain the workings of the universe. There are different branches of science, such as biology, physics, chemistry, and earth science. Each of these is further divided into more specific areas such as zoology and botany, both "twigs" on the biology branch.

■ *How do scientists find out about the world?* The "scientific method" is a process that scientists follow while studying and experimenting. It involves gathering information through observation, investigation, and experimentation. An important aspect of the scientific method is the idea of verifying information, or testing it for reliability. Observations and experiments are repeated over and over before stating findings as facts. Even then it's expected that other scientists may question the findings. This process of testing and

questioning adds an element of excitement to scientific study, as new discoveries are always just around the corner.

■ *How is science currently taught in schools?* In recent years, science educators have come to value the "let's find out together" approach that early childhood educators have always used with children. They're teaching school-aged children how to find out and how to use information — in short, how to do what scientists do. A program that provides young children with opportunities to experiment offers an excellent foundation for the discovery process they'll use in elementary school.

■ *What kinds of science experiences are developmentally appropriate for young children?* A concrete, hands-on approach to science is best suited to the learning styles of young children. At the same time, an effective science program grows out of and builds on children's innate desire to find out about their world. It also takes into account children's ages and stages — the differences in how young children approach experiences, depending on their age and developmental level. See "Ages and Stages in the Science Center," beginning on page 7, for guidance in planning activities for different ages.

Whatever their age, always remember children's need for active involvement in learning. Even when safety factors limit hands-on exploration, such as when cooking or when studying animals, look for ways children can actively participate, such as mixing ingredients or helping to feed the gerbils.

■ *How does the whole child benefit from science experiences?* At every age, but especially with young children, science activities do more than just stimulate cognitive learning. All areas of a child's development — social, emotional, physical, cognitive, and creative — benefit from science explorations.

Socially, young children get repeated opportunities to share materials, ideas, and observations with others. Many experiments require an extra pair of hands to be most successful. In a science setting, cooperative skills bloom naturally.

Emotionally, science activities offer rich potential for developing self-esteem as children make discoveries and complete explorations on their own. Learning about natural phenomena or creatures that can seem "scary" may also help children understand and conquer their fears. Expressing wonder and excitement adds delightfully satisfying moments for everyone, especially young children.

Physically, young children enhance their fine-motor coordination as they manipulate magnets, fill containers with water and sand, and perform a myriad of other small and large movements that are part of the process of experimentation.

Cognitively, children use a range of skills — such as problem-solving, math, and language — as they observe, predict, explore, test, quantify, and communicate. As children make discoveries about their world, their knowledge base builds.

Creatively, science lets children exercise their imaginative impulses. Through the process of finding out, children can experiment with new ideas or new ways to use tools and materials just to "see what happens if ... " Far from a rigid experience, science explorations are some of the most creative that children can participate in and enjoy. (For more benefits of science experiences, turn to the chart, "Learning and Growing Through Science," pages 22-25.)

HELPING CHILDREN UNDERSTAND SCIENCE

Children don't always recognize that many everyday activities and investigations are really science in action. When Al discovers a new way to make bubbles or Bethany brings in a collection of favorite rocks, that's science. You can help children make these important

connections and build on those events.

Early firsthand experiences with concrete materials and activities provide children with a strong foundation for later understanding of abstract scientific concepts. Four-year-old Noah is fascinated by watching water move up and down in his U-shaped tube as he lifts first one side, then another. A few years from now, it will be easier for him to understand the concept "water seeks its own level" because his understanding has been grounded in real experience. Even two-year-old Marguerite's experiences on the swing and seesaw may later help her to grasp physics concepts about balance, levers, and motion.

Share these important connections between everyday experiences and science concepts with family members, too. Give them the knowledge they need to recognize and build on science experiences at home. (Turn to "Sharing the Wonder of Science With Families," page 33, for ideas.)

PLANNING AND ORGANIZING FOR SCIENCE DISCOVERIES

You know that young children don't learn by being told. They need to make their own discoveries. But this process of finding out isn't haphazard. To be sure children get opportunities to explore, plan for science experiences. These ideas can help.

■ *Designate a special place in your room for science materials and activities.* Set up a science discovery area that encourages children to be independent and promotes self-directed learning. Organize it to encourage exploration and discovery. Make it safe, comfortable, and inviting. (For more guidance, turn to "Setting Up for Science," pages 28-32).

■ *Give children opportunities to explore in depth.* Schedule long, relaxed times to explore. Make sure you have enough materials so children don't have to wait

play as a way of processing new information and understanding complex concepts. Fact and fantasy often interweave; for example, "scientists" at the water table may mix "magic potions" and devise elaborate "inventions."

■ begin to understand what it means to experiment and become more purposeful and inventive in their explorations. They generally prefer their own experiments to those directed by an adult.

■ begin to select the activities they want to try ahead of time. In the science center, they will think through an activity, such as planting a seed, before they begin.

■ begin to make predictions based on their experiences.

■ like to think of explanations for what they observe, often embellishing fact with fantasy.

■ enjoy working with other children and begin to spontaneously share and take turns. They're comfortable in groups of four or five, with some adult guidance.

■ enjoy talking with others as they play and experiment. They like to learn new words and to play with language. They may have trouble speaking as fast as they think. Some stammering and stuttering are normal when children are excited.

■ begin to use drawings to represent and communicate ideas.

■ are gaining a strong awareness of written language. They enjoy dictating to adults and like to try writing on their own.

■ like to look at books, pretend to read, and talk about the pictures. They enjoy factual picture-reference books.

Five-year-olds:

- may design their own experiments to find out "what will happen if ... ," then brainstorm explanations for what they have observed (though they're not yet able to use true abstract reasoning and logic).
- can follow three-step directions and enjoy some teacher-directed experiments, along with plenty of open-ended ones.
- have long attention spans for activities they enjoy and may extend projects over several days.
- work cooperatively with five or six children. Sometimes help is needed to insure they listen to each other's ideas and share leadership.
- are interested in factual reference books with many illustrations. They may look through books for pictures that identify real objects they have observed, such as flowers.
- are quite verbal, though they may have trouble with some sounds. They enjoy conversation, but whole-group discussion may still be difficult because it's hard to wait for turns. Talks and problem-solving activities are most successful in small groups.
- have lots of information about some subjects without real understanding. They may try to grasp abstract concepts, but they still need concrete experiences.
- like to use drawing and writing to record their experiences.

too long for turns. Offer repeated experiences with the kinds of science materials and activities they love, such as sand and water.

When introducing new materials, give children plenty of time for random exploration and experimenting on their own before offering suggestions or setting up directed tasks.

■ *Offer children a wide range of science experiences.* Plan curriculum that includes:

- focusing on plants, animals, and people
- direct experiences with raw earth materials such as sand, soil, and water
- materials for manipulation, such as magnets, pulleys, water pumps, and waterwheels
- opportunities to observe changes, such as charting the growth of plants, animals, and children, and noting transformations during cooking experiences.

For more help with developing science curriculum themes and with defining concepts and activities, turn to "Exploring Science: Hands-On Themes for Young Scientists," pages 14-21.

■ *Observe children to find out which science experiences will interest them.* Use observation as the basis for planning science activities. General observations will help you determine children's interests, abilities, favorite activities, and levels of understanding of various scientific concepts. Observing in the science area will help you decide when to change an activity or when to extend one in a new way — such as moving from a general focus on dinosaurs to studying the teeth of meat-eaters and plant-eaters with fours or investigating bones and skeletons with fives. Develop curriculum around topics that you know are exciting to your children and that will elicit the greatest involvement.

■ *Plan for a balance of both open-ended and directed science experiences.*

There are basically three types of science experiences: open-ended, teacher-directed, and spontaneous. While you'll want open-ended and spontaneous experiences to dominate, there will be times when a directed activity that relates in a meaningful way to something children are curious about can extend learning in exciting ways.

Open-ended: In this type of activity, children are free to use the materials in their own ways. Organize materials for them to explore — such as setting out a tray of unbreakable magnifying and reducing lenses — but try not to have a particular outcome in mind.

This kind of creative exploration is essential. Children need to explore before trying more directed activities. Provide lots of open-ended activities and materials that suggest many possibilities. For example, set out a dishpan of sand and a variety of containers. As children mature, continue to provide open-ended activities but also challenge them to solve problems or to look for specific answers.

Teacher-directed: In this type of activity you may ask small groups to observe the same thing or work with the same materials, then invite them to share their reactions and ideas. In other words, you have an objective in mind for what children will gain from the activity, such as learning properties of objects that stick to magnets and properties of those that don't.

The key to successful directed activities is relating them to children's own experiences. For instance, you might introduce a more directed experience with magnets when one child has discovered through free exploration that a metal comb sticks to the magnet but a plastic one won't; or introduce an activity about air when a child asks on a windy day, "What is wind?"

Spontaneous: These unplanned experiences can be some of the most satisfying for children because they reflect their interests and are triggered by specific events. For example, an unplanned experience might be spotting worms above ground during an after-rain walk. Depending on your group and particulars of the event, you might just observe together, follow up with a more directed activity, and/or share a special book. The important thing is to be alert to the "teachable moments" in everyday life. These offer opportunities to observe, to wonder, and to further investigate cause and effect, such as pointing out the ice that has replaced yesterday's puddle.

TEACHING CHILDREN SCIENTISTS' SKILLS

As children engage in science experiences, they don't need to learn facts. They need to find out and use information creatively and productively. Just like real scientists, children need to use process skills — observing, classifying, quantifying, predicting, experimenting, and communicating — as they explore. Helping children develop these skills will enhance their enjoyment of science.

■ *Observing* — Observation is key to all science activities. Children can learn to be good observers as you help them use *all* of their senses. Ask what they see, hear, smell, taste, and feel. Focus their observations by having them look for specific objects. Then help them look for traits and characteristics of those objects, such as size, shape, texture, color, etc. Encourage children to look for change, one of the most important conditions scientists watch for.

■ *Classifying* — Classifying is a necessary skill in understanding how things in the world, from plants to machines, are grouped together by certain traits. Children learn to classify by first noticing differences and similarities. Very young children can match identical pairs of objects or pictures. Eventually they learn to sort objects that are similar but not identical; for example, objects of similar shape or color. As children mature, they begin to understand that objects can belong to more than one category at a time.

Children often group objects according to their own categories, rather than ones adults might expect. Remember that there is no right or wrong way to sort a group of objects. The objective is to get children to identify why something does or does not belong in a group.

■ *Quantifying* — Counting, measuring, weighing, estimating, and comparing differences in size, space, and distance are all quantifying skills that children use as they experiment and explore. Offer younger children opportunities to judge *more* or *less*, *larger* or *smaller*, *shorter* or *taller*, etc. Older children can begin to find out *how long* and *how far*, and then *how much more* or *how much less*.

■ *Predicting* — The ability to predict what might happen based on past experiences is not only a critical science skill but an important life skill. It's one that develops with practice, so offer children lots of opportunities to make predictions. Even twos can make simple guesses about familiar activities: "What might happen if I touch the bubble?" At a more advanced level, a child might generalize that an untried object made of wood won't stick to his or her magnet because other wooden objects haven't in the past.

■ *Experimenting* — This is the skill most commonly associated with sci-ence. For young children, its development begins with open-ended exploration. They need opportunities to experience random exploration with materials — that may or may not lead to identifiable discoveries — before they are asked to follow adult directions. From this free exploration, they will, on their own, begin to direct their experiments in a more deliberate and purposeful way and may try out each other's experiments. Only then are children really ready for teacher-directed experiments.

■ *Communicating* — An important part of any science experience is sharing one's findings with others. Help young children use words to describe, explain, and discuss their activities. Introduce appropriate science vocabulary for their experiences. For example, talk about *friction* when a bare-legged child gets stuck on the slide or *suction* as children fill a meat baster at the water table. Explore with children a variety of ways to record observations and experiences, such as on experience charts, on graphs, or in drawings and photographs. Use demonstrations and displays as ways to share with others.

FOLLOWING THE CHILD'S LEAD

Again, as you focus and guide children's explorations, take care not to be

SCIENCE WITH MIXED AGE GROUPS

The spontaneous discoveries that make science so exciting happen all the time in the home setting of a family day-care program. Simple experiences like helping tend the garden, cooking lunch, watching the repair-person fix the washing machine, or huddling on your lap when thunder cracks offer rich opportunities to explore science in everyday ways. Children can observe change, see how things work, and talk about confusing or frightening elements in the natural world.

Working with children who represent a mix of ages also poses special challenges. Here are ways to insure that science experiences are safe, successful, and appropriate for all of the children in your care.

■ *Plan for safety.* Many materials and activities that are safe for older children may be hazardous for younger

too directive or dominating. Use observation as a guide for interacting with children. Watch what they are trying to do and find out on their own, before you interrupt. By observing closely, you can take your cues from the children and decide whether, when, and how to step in with a comment, question, suggestion, demonstration, offer of help, or additional materials.

If you wish to join children in an activity, you might ask if they need an assistant to hold something. In this role you can often indirectly suggest ideas or new directions. For example, you might ask children if they would like you to do something or get another piece of equipment for them to try. Some children will not want you to join or help them, and it is important to respect their wishes.

■ *Encourage children to talk about what they are doing.* Talking with children informally as they work and play is a good way to learn more about what they are experiencing. When you understand how much the children understand, you can more easily plan activities to extend their learning.

■ *Ask questions to stimulate thinking and experimentation.* Encourage children to make predictions, estimate, and suggest explanations for what they observe. Use open-ended questions — the kind that allow for *many* possible answers — to invite a wide range of responses or to elicit opinions. Questions that only allow for right or wrong answers will turn off children's flow of ideas and creative thinking. Children who are "wrong" too many times soon become afraid to risk any answers at all.

Open-ended questions such as "I wonder where that ice on the steps came from? Does anyone have an idea?" invite children to brainstorm as many ideas as possible. This type of questioning can lead children into animated discussions. Then, instead of telling children a "correct" answer, you can point out that they have given many different answers, some of which contradict each other. This might be a good time to explain that scientists often have different opinions, and that's why they do lots of experiments to find out their answers. Follow with another important open-ended question: "How do you think we could find out?"

Thus challenged, children will be eager to try out their own experiments and research their own answers — which, of course, is what you really want them to do!

---

ones. When planning, keep the following ideas in mind.
• Be sure older children's workspaces are out of reach of babies and toddlers. Help older children remember to clean up when they finish science activities, checking that small items, such as paper clips used with a magnet or small stones, have not fallen on the floor where a younger child might find and swallow them.
• Include little children in some activities by offering similar but safer materials. For example, let older children work with small magnets and younger children with larger ones.

■ *Encourage multiage activities.* Offer as many activities as possible that can be enjoyed by everyone, such as a walk to look for animals or color-mixing with paints and food coloring. Focus on open-ended free exploration of materials like water, sand, and soil, so that children of different ages can enjoy materials, do investigations, and make discoveries in their own ways.

■ *Ask age-appropriate questions to focus observations and stretch children's thinking.* Observing together lets children focus on their interests and on what they can identify, but still learn from the observations of others. For example, when watching an animal, ask toddlers if the animal has eyes and a mouth. Threes can look for toes, tails, or whiskers. Fours and fives could count feet or look for fur, feathers, and scales. School-aged children might identify features that help the animal adapt to the environment.

Ideas contributed by Susan Bromberg Kleinsinger and Kathie Spitzley.

EXPLORING SCIENCE:
HANDS-ON THEMES FOR YOUNG SCIENTISTS

How do you choose science themes to explore with young children? Ideally, you don't actually choose as much as offer interesting materials. Let children make their own discoveries as you guide experiences that broaden their exposure to and understanding of the world.

In this section you'll find eight basic topics: life-science studies of animals, plants, and people; earth-science studies of air, water, sand, and soil; and physical-science studies of magnets and simple machines. These by no means exhaust the range of science investigations to enjoy with children. But they are familiar themes that build on what children know and introduce new ideas to pique children's interest about mysteries they've yet to uncover.

The suggested themes and activities for each topic just touch the surface of possible explorations. You and your children will discover many others. For activities related to these and other science topics, turn to the Activity Plans on pages 38-77.

LIFE SCIENCES: ANIMALS, PLANTS, AND PEOPLE
ANIMAL ADVENTURES

Be it a cuddly bunny, wiggly worm, or ferocious shark, children are curious about animals. Experiences with appropriate animals broaden children's knowledge and understanding. Sharing responsibility for the well-being of a pet helps children gain respect for all life.

Themes and Activities

■ **Observing animals** — Provide direct experiences. Take walks to look for animals outdoors. Plan trips to zoos or wildlife parks. Remember, children need in-depth experiences, which caring for a pet can provide. Select a pet you can care for easily. Together, find out as much as possible about the animal and its needs. Set up a rotating job chart to ensure that each interested child has opportunities to care for the pet.

■ **Animal environments** — Aquariums and terrariums let children observe animals in settings similar to their natural habitats. Join children as they observe. Ask questions to focus observation and thinking skills: "What do you think helps the black fish swim?" "How do you think fish swim so fast?" "Can fish swim backwards? How can we find out?"

■ **Animal babies** — Young children are often intrigued by young animals. Together, find out what different babies look like and what newborn animals can do. Does the animal parent feed, protect, and teach the offspring, as human parents do? Try to measure and record the growth of live animals.

■ **Animal movements** — Observing and imitating animal movements is a favorite activity of young children. Use this theme for music and movement and creative dramatic activities.

■ **Animal characteristics** — Help children observe features that identify different animals. Focus on how animals and people are alike and different, then compare certain animals to other animals. Which ones have fur, feathers, skin, or scales? Which have whiskers or tails? Children use these comparisons as they learn to group animals.

Remember

■ Examine your own attitudes toward less-popular creatures like snakes, spiders, and mice. Be careful not to limit children's experiences with some animals because of your feelings. At the same time, remember that children need to learn which animals should be avoided or handled with caution.

■ Support and guide children as they interact with live animals. Learn the proper way to hold an animal. Show children, giving both the animal and the children your full attention.

PLANT EXPLORATIONS

As you know, plants are an integral part of our world. We eat and use plant products. Plants prevent soil erosion and contribute oxygen to the air. Many animals depend on plants for food and shelter. Help children learn how plants affect their own lives and how to care for them.

Themes and Activities

■ **Caring for plants** — Nurturing plants can be deeply satisfying for children, giving them feelings of responsibility and competence. They learn that plants have needs — air, light, water, nutrients — and what happens if some needs aren't met.

■ **Plants outdoors** — To really learn about plants, children need to observe them in natural environments. Start with a basic: Observe grass growing on lawns, in fields, or pushing through concrete cracks. Collect and press leaves that have fallen from trees. Select a tree to visit regularly and observe changes with the seasons. Plant

a young tree in the schoolyard to observe its growth.

Start an outdoor garden. Plant bulbs in fall, then flower seeds in spring. Visit public gardens. Ask family members who are gardeners to assist with your planting projects. As you garden and explore together, help instill in children your own respect for the environment as you encourage their sense of wonder.

■ **Investigating seeds** — Collect and look at seeds from outdoors. Observe the ways seeds travel — by water, by wind, on animals, etc. Save seeds from fruits and vegetables, then compare for similarities and differences. Display seeds with pictures of the foods they come from. Together, investigate which foods have the most seeds. Do foods of the same kind have the same number of seeds? Explore and sample edible seeds, such as peanuts, popcorn, and pumpkin seeds.

■ **Sprouting seeds** — Help children understand that the same kinds of seeds always produce the same kinds of plants. Look for baby plants hiding inside seeds. Soak dry lima beans overnight, then carefully pull the two halves apart to find the curled-up plant

WALKS WITHOUT WORRY

A nature walk can be a delightful experience for all ages. Children love the opportunity to get outside and explore. With a little prior scouting and a few simple reminders, you can make both planned and impromptu treks more satisfying and fun!

■ Check out your neighborhood before your walk. Decide on good, safe routes with lots to see. Avoid high-traffic areas and busy streets. Watch for poison ivy, poison oak, and plants that may aggravate allergies.

■ To avoid the pitfall of taking a walk "to look for animals," then finding none, search for animals children are likely to see. Remember, many creatures are nocturnal or will be frightened away by noisy preschoolers. Know where birds, squirrels, and insects — those most likely to accept pint-sized observers — reside. Or take a walk to look for signs of animals: feathers, fur, nests, chewed leaves or bark, etc.

■ Keep an extra change of clothing for each child in case walks get "messy." This way you won't miss out on a chance to explore in a light rain.

■ Take along a portable first-aid kit, just in case. Note whether bees are out in full force and keep a special eye on children who are allergic to bee sting.

■ Don't worry if you can't identify every tree, cloud, or caterpillar that children observe. Remember, finding out together is half the fun. Just make the next walk a trip to the library!

embryo. Plant lima beans, experimenting with different growing mediums, such as sand, soil, and water. Sprout beans on damp paper towels, blotter paper, cotton, or sponges so children can see both roots and stems growing.

■ **Reproduction from cuttings and roots** — Take cuttings from house plants and compare how they grow in soil and in water. Cut off the tops of carrots, onions, and pineapples to grow on pebbles in a shallow dish of water. Cut pieces of root from plants, such as mint, to grow in soil.

Remember

■ Some plants are poisonous if they are ingested, or cause allergic reactions. Know these plants and avoid them, but also keep first-aid information and hotline numbers on hand for emergencies.

■ Children often overwater plants. Limit the amount by using basters, misters, or sprayers.

■ To keep plants from drying out over weekends or vacations, make a loose "greenhouse" tent over plants with plastic. Place in a spot with indirect sun and water well.

■ Prepare for seeds and plants that won't survive by having more than one plant per child and some communal plants. Approach planting activities with an experimental attitude: "I wonder which ones will sprout."

ALL ABOUT ME AND YOU

Children want to know about their bodies — how they work, what's inside, what can happen to them, and how they're alike and different from other children.

Themes and Activities

■ **What's on the outside?** Children are beginning to understand that their **skin** protects the inside of their bodies and keeps blood from coming out. They are trying to understand differences in skin color and may wonder if theirs will change, especially if they're aware of tanning. At the same time, they may have noticed that skin is absorbent. (You can use materials such as baby lotion and baby oil on their hands to compare which absorbs more easily and which makes their hands waterproof.)

Children are curious about **injuries** to their skin, such as cuts, scrapes, and bruises. Let them watch as you help a child with a minor injury. Observe the different stages as a scrape heals to help children understand how the body can help itself. Listen to their feelings and respect their fears. Discuss ways to keep our bodies safe and healthy.

Hair is another fascination. Young children like to feel hair that is different from theirs. Compare one another's hair textures and colors, expressing out loud that everyone's hair is different and that's okay. You can also compare human hair to the fur of familiar animals. Look at the diversity of colors and patterns in hair and fur. Talk about the purpose of each.

■ **What's on the inside?** Children like to feel their **bones** and compare what they feel with pictures or toy skeletons. Focus on joints through creative movement activities. Explore the different directions joints can move. Ask, "How many ways can your wrist move? Which ways can you bend your knees?"

Teeth are also fascinating, especially to fives who may be losing some. Ask a dentist for models of teeth to examine.

Young children are very aware of their own growing strength and like to show off their arm **muscles**. Help them recognize that they have muscles all over and that each kind of muscle does different work. Invite children to explore: "What do finger muscles do? Which muscles do you use to pull, push, lift, and carry? What muscles do you use to jump? Can you feel muscles moving when you chew?"

■ **How do you grow and change?** Young children love to help measure and record their own growth. (Avoid comparisons between children by keeping personal charts that show how much

each child has grown since the last measurement.) How else can children tell they've grown? Children are especially interested in how they've changed since they were babies and in comparing their abilities to those of babies. Ask children to bring in pictures of themselves as babies. Invite some babies to visit your group. Talk about what preschool-aged children can do that babies aren't able to do yet.

Remember

■ Discussion of the human body can naturally lead to questions about reproduction and also about death. Parents may have strong feelings about what's said to their children on these subjects. Work with them to decide what information to share.

■ Help children understand that differences in skin and hair color, body size, temperament, and behavior are normal and natural. Show that you value and care about each child as a unique being. Also emphasize the ways in which all people are alike.

EARTH SCIENCES: AIR, WATER, SAND, AND SOIL

INVESTIGATING AIR

Sometimes we can't feel air, and other times it can pluck off hats, bend trees, even knock down a wall. Help children learn more about the mysterious air they breathe.

Themes and Activities

■ **Air is all around us.** Try experiments indoors to test for air. Ask children to wave their arms to feel air tickle their skin, and suck air in to observe how their cheeks, chest, and stomach swell. Then ask them to exhale and listen for sounds as they blow air out of their bodies.

■ **Air moves.** Use dry basters, eyedroppers, pumps, and squirt bottles to find ways to make air move. Have children squeeze and pump, aiming at their own cheeks and hands. What do they feel? Where do they think the air comes from? If they push air out, how does more air get in? Try blowing air under water. What happens? Where do the bubbles come from? What do we call moving air outdoors?

■ **Air can move objects.** Experiment to see how air can move light objects such as ping-pong balls, feathers, and tissue-paper scraps. Ask children to blow with their mouths, blow through straws, and wave paper fans. What do they think makes the objects move? Which methods work best?

Remember

- Build on children's interests. If some children are curious about windmills, for example, talk about how people harness the wind to do work.
- Children who have been in a hurricane or tornado may need to share their fears about the wind.

WATER WONDERS

As you know, water is one of the most common yet precious resources. It makes up most of the earth's surface and most of our own bodies. Without it, all life would perish. From their earliest experiences, children have been learning about water. Build on their interest and pleasure in water to help them discover more about it.

Themes and Activities

- **How does water move?** Encourage experimentation by providing a variety of plastic containers with openings of different sizes. Add a few drops of food coloring so children can see more clearly what happens as water moves. Offer items for squirting and spraying, such as basters, misters, and eyedroppers. Add funnels and tubes, so children can connect objects and create their own waterworks.

- **Water takes many forms.** Help children understand the changes water goes through as it moves from a liquid to a gaseous state. Provide sprayers, misters, and atomizers so children can experiment.

Try aiming sprays and mists into the air. Relate these to **mist** and **fog** children have seen and felt outdoors. Also, boil a little water in a clear glass pot, and let children watch from a safe distance. Can they see the level of the water getting lower? Talk about **steam**. Explain that heat can make water into such tiny droplets they can't even be seen. Relate these experiences to what children know about **evaporation**.

On a rainy day, go outside to observe the **rain**. How does it feel? How does it look? How does it sound on different surfaces? On a wintry day, catch **snowflakes** on dark cloth and examine with a magnifying glass. Explain that snow forms from something similar to the mist and steam children have observed. Invite children to blow on an icy cold window to observe as **frost** forms. Scrape frost from the inside of a freezer and view it through a magnifying lens.

Let children tell you what they know about **ice**. Make ice together to confirm their understandings, then let it melt back to water.

- **What floats, what sinks?** Children have seen objects float and sink since they played with their first bathtub toys. Help them express what they know and challenge them to experiment further. Sit with children as they play. At appropriate moments, ask questions and call attention to discoveries: "That swirled to the bottom? I wonder which other objects will do the same thing. What do you think?" Provide a variety of boats and encourage children to note if they all float in the same way. What does it take to sink one? Start a list of "water words" to add to from conversations during water play.

Remember

- Rather than expecting children to fully understand many concepts related to water, such as evaporation, offer them *experiences*. In time, observing and hands-on testing will lead to conceptual understanding.
- Encourage children to talk, question, and wonder.

EXPLORING SAND AND SOIL

Whether at the beach or in the backyard, sand and soil fascinate children. They want to dig in it, feel it, mold it, and look for the living and nonliving treasures found in it. Building on this innate interest leads children to greater understanding of these resources.

Themes and Activities

- **What is soil made of?** Set up an area outdoors with tools and utensils chil-

FIELD-TRIP TIPS

A good field trip offers the kind of direct experience that young children are excited by and find most meaningful, but it also requires planning. The first step is deciding where to go.

PLACES TO GO: DOS AND DON'TS

▪ *Museums* — Hands-on children's museums are the best choice for all ages. Fours and fives may enjoy brief, focused visits to natural-history museums, but you will need to prepare children for what they'll see. Remember, some children may be confused by mounted animals and preoccupied with why and how the animals died. Exhibits of dinosaur skeletons can be very disappointing if children expect the creatures they see in books.

▪ *Planetariums* — Even when children show interest in space, they're not always ready for this kind of visit. Most shows are too long, so look for programs specifically designed for children five and under, or save this trip until they're older.

▪ *Zoos, Aquariums, and Wildlife Centers* — Visit ahead of time to be sure animals are cared for properly, kept in natural settings, and protected from exploitation and abuse.

▪ *Botanical Gardens, Parks, and Preserves* — Check ahead of time to find out what kinds of plants and trees you'll see and what will be in bloom at the time of your visit. Plan games and activities to focus observations and to make the experience interactive.

GETTING READY

The best way to prepare for any kind of field trip is to visit your destination ahead of time. Even if you know the site from a personal outing, make this scouting visit with your children in mind. Decide what to see, how long to spend in each place, and how to get from place to place. Note also the location of restrooms and cafeterias, as well as any safety hazards to avoid. Be sure to inquire about rules.

FOCUS THE VISIT

Plan related activities in advance of the visit. Encourage children to ask questions and to decide what they want to find out and look for during the visit.

PLAN FOR ADEQUATE SUPERVISION

Enlist the help of enough adults so that each is responsible for only a few children. Familiarize all adults with the plans for the day. Review safety rules, including a plan for meeting if the group is separated. Provide chaperones with a map of the area (including restrooms) and open-ended questions to share with children that relate to the theme of the visit.

REVIEW SAFETY RULES

Provide durable name tags for children labeled with school name, address, and phone number. (For safety from strangers, don't put the children's names on the tags.) For identification purposes, you might have children wear a special color or a T-shirt with the school name. Wear something yourself that will help you to pop out in a crowd. Review safety rules with everyone before you depart.

Bring along a first-aid kit, money for emergency transportation, and the daytime number of a family member for each child. Be sure someone at school has the phone number of the destination and is available if you need to call for help.

ACTIVITIES FOR ON THE ROAD

If travel will be longer than 15 minutes, bring along materials to keep children occupied, such as books and magazines, preferably related to the field-trip theme. Or share familiar songs and fingerplays. As children are seated on the bus or van, consider pairing up those who are less likely to overstimulate each other.

FOLLOW-UP FUN

Following your visit, take time to share reactions and stories. Send a note to families telling what you saw and offering suggestions for related activities to do at home. During the year, talk about the visit any time a related activity develops. If interest is high, you might even plan a repeat visit. Young children become more confident learners as their familiarity with a subject grows.

SAFETY
FIVE STEPS TO SCIENCE SAFETY

The science area and science explorations pose their share of risks. There are harmful materials to beware of, small objects to keep out of the reach of younger children, and animals or insects that may scratch or bite when eager observers get too close. To maintain safety, follow these five important steps.

■ **Know the risks.** Some potential problems are obvious. For example, you know twos taste everything, so it's important to never give them small objects they might swallow. Twos get the big magnets to work with, the big objects to test.

Seek out information from experts who can alert you to other dangers of which you're less aware. For example, a local greenhouse or the botany department at a nearby college could help identify plants which are nontoxic and plants which require your careful supervision. A veterinarian or zoology teacher could identify safe animals to keep in your room and explain "dos" and "don'ts" for handling them. Many science publications also offer valuable safety information.

■ **Give materials a safety check.** Before you put out an old appliance for children to take apart, cut off the cord and look for gears or gadgets with sharp edges. Check batteries and thermometers for

dren can use to dig. As they explore, encourage them to note textures, colors, and smells. What is soil made of? Can they find bits of decaying plants that add nutrients to soil? Is all soil alike?

Before planting activities, let children examine and play with potting soil. How do they think it differs from playground soil?

■ **What is sand made of?** Bring a magnifying lens to the sandbox for close-up views. What do children see? Help them identify bits of stone, shell, and coral. Provide sand of different colors and coarseness for comparison. Add water to dry sand so children can compare. How does each feel? What happens when you try to pour each? Is one easier to build with than the other?

■ **Let's collect stones, rocks, and shells.** What adults see as dirty pebbles, children see as precious gems. Be prepared for ardent collectors by setting up a miniature rock museum. Together, note the amazing variety of shapes, colors, and textures. Look for bits of stone in soil to help children understand that part of soil comes from broken-down stone. Encourage them to sort by size, texture, color, or a scheme they devise.

If you are near a beach or have children who have visited one, invite them to bring in shells they've collected and provide others children can handle and sort. Talk about how shells break into small bits and become parts of the sand and about the sea animals that once lived in the shells and used the hard surface as protection.

Remember
■ Before children play outdoors, check soil for bits of broken glass or other hazards. Before bringing soil indoors, check for unwanted "guests" better left outdoors. At the same time, use this experience to remind children of the many creatures that make their homes in soil.
■ Remind children to wash their hands after playing in sand or soil.

PHYSICAL SCIENCE: MAGNETS AND MACHINES
MANIPULATING MAGNETS

Magnets invite children to manipulate, experiment, and invent. With a myriad of possibilities for exploration and discovery, they encourage practice of a range of science process skills. These concrete experiences also lay the foundation for children to grasp abstract concepts of energy and force.

Themes and Activities
■ **Experiment with energy, force, and power.** Many children are fascinated by a magnet's invisible energy. Sometimes two magnets stick together and are hard to pull apart; sometimes they push each other away. As children use their own energy to resist the magnets' force, they sense their own strength and control.

Start children with random exploration of magnets of various sizes and shapes. Work with just the magnets, so children can focus on the power of the magnets pushing and pulling. Talk about other experiences they've had with pushing and pulling — such as using their own energy to move things or watching machines at work — to help children see the magnet's power as a kind of energy.

■ **All magnets aren't the same.** Set out magnets of various strengths, along with materials such as metal paper clips and juice lids. Encourage children to compare magnets and arrive at the conclusion on their own that some are stronger than others. They may also discover that the more magnets they put together, the more things they can pick up.

■ **Let's experiment with magnetic attraction.** When children are really familiar with magnets, add assorted objects made of metal, wood, cloth, string, rubber, and plastic. Let children experiment freely. Provide "yes" and "no" baskets with picture labels for sorting materials by those that stick and those that don't. Challenge them to sort objects first, then to use the magnets to check predictions.

Remember

- Carefully supervise very young children when using small magnets.
- To prevent loss, use small magnets on trays. Provide large magnets for exploration around the room.
- Encourage children to use their own words to describe observations and discoveries. Introduce terms such as *attract* and *repel* when children have experienced these reactions.

LEARNING ABOUT SIMPLE MACHINES

Levers, pendulums, ramps, pulleys, and wheels are all **simple machines**. Playground equipment such as the seesaw (lever), slide (ramp), and swing (pendulum) are simple machines in your own schoolyard. Through experiences with simple machines, children develop awareness of such physics concepts as weight, gravity, balance, and leverage.

Themes and Activities

- **Levers** — The seesaw offers an ideal lesson in how levers work. As children play, talk about how balance is affected by differences in weight and by moving closer to or farther away from the center. Offer many opportunities for children to dig with shovels and they will learn that the heavier the load to lift, the harder they have to push down on the handle.

- **Pendulums** — Give children time to swing and they will be learning about pendulums, discovering how much energy they need to exert and how to angle their bodies to make the swing go higher. They will also feel how hard it is to stop the swing once it's moving.

- **Ramps** — Children learn from slides, from riding toys, and from their play with toy vehicles that the steeper the incline of a ramp, the faster an object will travel down it. And when going up a ramp, a steeper incline requires more energy.

- **Pulleys** — Set up a clothesline pulley outdoors or indoors so children can experience how pulleys make moving and lifting things easier. Provide a basket children can attach to send light loads across the yard or room. Together, rig up a pulley and rope over an indoor digging area, then invite children to load, hoist, and dump pails of sand or soil.

- **Wheels** — Wheels are powered in different ways. Some move with a push. Some wind up. Ask parents to save broken wind-up toys so children can see the mechanisms inside. Save wheels from broken toys for children to play with or use in making "inventions." Together, take a closer look at how tricycles and other riding toys are made. Talk about what powers them and how the parts move and interact.

- **Science and dramatic play** — Save appliances that no longer work for children to take apart with child-sized tools in a "repair shop" or "inventor's workshop." *Check to be sure there are no dangerous parts, and cut off cords before giving to children.* As children take on pretend roles, they learn more about simple machines through their own investigations.

Remember

- Complex machines are developed from simple machines. Observing real machines that employ combinations of levers, pulleys, and wheels, as well as playing with toy dump trucks, derricks, and cranes, lead to an understanding of how machines work.
- Working with machines and tools requires close supervision. Choose tools and materials that are appropriate for your group. Teach children how to use, carry, and care for tools safely. With very young children, watch out for small parts.
- While children don't need to know the technical words for scientific principles, some fours and fives may want to know words like *lever* and *leverage*. Share words as children show interest in science vocabulary.

cracks and leaks. Provide plastic objects and unbreakable mirrors. If you're not sure whether a tool or material is safe for children to use, don't bring it into your science center.

- **Know your children.** Some children are more likely than others to take risks. Get to know who's most likely to taste-test plants, seeds, etc.; who may not listen to warnings about careful use of tools and materials; and who's most likely to pinch the guinea pig to see what it does. This way you can anticipate problems before they arise.

- **Supervise carefully.** This is the real key to safety. Observe what children are doing and how they're using materials and equipment. Sometimes frequent but casual observation is enough. But whenever children are engaged in potentially problematic activities, such as using a heat source to observe changes, observing with a glass prism or lens, handling an animal, or planting bulbs or seeds that are harmful if sampled, work alongside them. Take charge when appropriate and let children observe from a safe distance. Be sure the size of the group is small enough that you know what everyone is doing at all times.

- **Review safety rules.** Be sure children understand why certain tools, materials, plants, and animals must be handled in certain ways. Safety rules should be simple, straightforward — and reviewed together every day!

LEARNING AND GROWING

BY SCOTT HEWIT, Ed.D.

Science activities are some of the most exciting, challenging, and satisfying experiences for young children. They're also some of the most well-rounded. This four-page chart illustrates the versatility of science explorations and how they can contribute to the development of the whole child — socially, emotionally, physically, cognitively, and creatively. It can be shared with teachers, with aides, and with children's families to help them recognize the richness of science.

Each entry begins with a description of how a specific skill or concept is developed through science experiences. "Ways to Assist" provides ideas for enhancing further development. "Developmental Considerations" will help you know what to expect from younger (ages 2-3) and older (ages 4-5) preschoolers.

Naturally, behavior varies greatly at any age. What individual children gain from science explorations also depends on factors such as prior experience with materials and concepts. Use the chart as a source of guidelines only.

THROUGH SCIENCE

COGNITIVE DEVELOPMENT

LANGUAGE SKILLS

Communicating observations and ideas about what and why something happened is an important science process skill. Classifying and predicting also require use of oral language, as does problem-solving, a frequent part of the discovery process. Children learn new vocabulary as they experience science in action. As they watch you record their dictated words, they see how written language is used to communicate ideas.

Ways to Assist
- Share new science words that relate to children's activities.
- Ask open-ended questions that require more than "yes" or "no" answers. Encourage children to describe their ideas.
- Give children paper and writing tools and model writing on experience charts.

Developmental Considerations
- Younger children may need help in telling about what they observe. Model language by describing children's actions.
- Older children can engage in small-group discussion where they share observations, predictions, and conclusions. They may want to dictate observations and responses or try writing on their own.

THINKING SKILLS

Open-ended science exploration encourages children to use a range of thinking skills. They make decisions about what tools and materials to use, tap prior knowledge as they predict what might happen, solve problems, classify information, and draw conclusions about what happened and why. Exciting discoveries and new information help to hone thinking skills.

Ways to Assist
- Make time for children to share what they know about a science topic to connect past experiences with present ones.
- Ask open-ended questions that urge children to think about many possible answers.
- Encourage children to find their own solutions to science problems. Let them test ideas, even if their logic is faulty.
- Invite children to share science experiences and ideas about what happened and why. You'll get a window on their thinking processes.

Developmental Considerations
- Younger children need time to explore their environment and opportunities to test objects to decide how they can be used. Thinking skills develop as twos and threes gain understanding of the world around them.
- Older children can engage in fairly complex reasoning because they have more experiences on which to draw when making predictions. Enhanced language skills help them articulate their thinking.

MATH SKILLS

Quantifying is also a science process skill. Most science activities involve some use of math skills, such as counting, measuring, comparing amounts, or graphing results. By introducing or reinforcing these concepts in a meaningful setting, you help children recognize early on that math has real use in everyday life, a critical understanding that can enhance later learning.

Ways to Assist
- Look for ways to incorporate math into science activities, such as measuring shadows, plants, and animals with string.
- Create simple graphs to help children compare quantities.
- Point out cases of one-to-one correspondence — one seed per cup, one magnet for each child, etc.
- Encourage children to use estimating skills: "About how many stones will fit in the can?"

Developmental Considerations
- Younger children are just developing an understanding of numbers. Their counting skills are limited to holding up two or three fingers to show their age.
- Older children may recite from one to 10 but may not have a firm concept of what those numerals represent. They compare quantities as being *more than* or *less than*, but judgments are based on appearance. They can measure to compare lengths of string, but they're not ready to use units such as inches.

LEARNING AND GROWING

CREATIVE DEVELOPMENT

CREATIVE EXPLORATION

If creativity involves using materials and thinking about situations in novel ways, then science activities are the perfect outlet for creative instincts. By emphasizing the process of finding out over memorizing facts, you offer children opportunities to form and to test imaginative responses to their own questions about how the world works.

Ways to Assist

- Encourage open-ended exploration and child-directed learning. Sincerely accept children's ideas to stimulate continued creativity.
- Offer materials that can be used in many ways and allow for a range of results.
- Let children test ideas and learn from their own mistakes.
- Occasionally challenge their creativity: "How do you think we could make this clay boat float?"

Developmental Considerations

- Younger children don't organize creative behavior in a systematic way, but positive feedback will encourage them to continue creative efforts.
- Older children can actually become more logical thinkers through creative exploration as they see results firsthand. They need time to evaluate their observations and, if not satisfied, to repeat activities.

SOCIAL/EMOTIONAL DEVELOPMENT

COOPERATING AND SHARING

Science activities encourage interaction between children in natural ways, so, as they experiment, children may want to enlist a buddy to help. In their excitement, they want to share discoveries with a friend. Emphasizing interrelationships in the natural world can be a bridge to focusing on the interrelationships among the children in your group.

Ways to Assist

- Look for ways to encourage teamwork through science activities. Praise children for working well together.
- Provide opportunities for children to share their ideas and experiences with others.
- Let children try to solve their own conflicts. Mediate to help them find solutions that work for everyone involved.

Developmental Considerations

- Younger children are egocentric so it is difficult for them to cooperate or share easily. Plan science activities where they can work parallel to others on the same project.
- Older children are learning to cooperate and like working with peers. They do best in small cooperative groups. Large-group activities are frustrating if they must wait long for turns.

DEVELOPING POSITIVE SELF-CONCEPTS

Directly and indirectly, science activities help children develop a positive view of themselves. Learning to respect all life enhances a child's own self-worth as he or she recognizes that everyone and everything has a place in the world. Investigating change in the natural world and in themselves helps reassure children that what they can't do today they may be able to do tomorrow, whenever their bodies say it's time.

Ways to Assist

- From worms to weeds, model respect for all living things.
- Celebrate individuality. Help children see that just as no two snowflakes are identical, no two children are exactly alike.
- Help children learn about their bodies and how they are growing and changing.
- Provide open-ended activities in the science center so children can work at their own pace and experience success in their own ways.

Developmental Considerations

- Younger children benefit from experiences that focus on themselves. They need to develop belief in their own abilities to achieve a sense of self.
- Older children are more aware of ways in which they are different from others. Their self-esteem can be delicate. Note individual children's strengths to insure that each child has chances to grow and to shine throughout the year.

THROUGH SCIENCE

PHYSICAL DEVELOPMENT

COPING WITH NATURE-RELATED FEARS

Snakes and spiders, thunder and lightning, even the dark of night can be very frightening to young children. Learning about these things can help children reach clearer understandings and diminish their fears. As mystery and fear are replaced by understanding and acceptance, children are helped to feel more secure in their world.

Ways to Assist
- Never belittle a child's fears of the natural world. Aim to decrease them through knowledge.
- Don't push a child to confront a fear, such as insisting that a frightened child touch a harmless snake. Encourage gradual exposure through books and discussion.
- Acknowledge that some creatures are dangerous. Teach appropriate safety rules.
- Consider your own nature-related fears and try not to pass them on.

Developmental Considerations
- Younger children are often fearful of violent storms. Rather than try to explain scientifically what's happening (the concepts are too abstract), provide much-needed warmth and security. However, in some situations, twos and threes can be notoriously fearless and will need constant supervision, especially outside.
- Older children benefit from information as a way to dispel fear. Understanding what is real and what is not is basic to relieving stress at this age.

SENSORY PERCEPTION

Children use their senses to gather information about the world. In fact, observing is one of the most important science process skills. Though most input comes from sight and hearing, the young child also relies on taste, touch, and smell. Observation skills, attention span, and curiosity are enhanced through conscious use of the five senses.

Ways to Assist
- Talk about the senses, pointing out distinctive sights, sounds, smells, textures, and tastes.
- Provide an unbreakable magnifying lens for close observations indoors and out.
- Sharpen each sense. Plan walks to focus on one sense — sounds, smells, sights, textures — at a time. Have a tasting party.

Developmental Considerations
- Younger children can be overwhelmed by too much sensory input. Keep your indoor environment subdued.
- Older children are more in tune with their senses and able to process information using several senses at once.

FINE-MOTOR SKILLS

Almost any science activity involves manipulating materials and using fine-motor skills. Balancing objects on a scale requires precision. Measuring a plant's height with a string takes eye-hand coordination. Using an eyedropper to water plants tests finger control. Science offers many ways to enhance fine-motor skills.

Ways to Assist
- Let children practice manipulating science tools freely before using them in activities and experiments.
- Provide a variety of tools of different sizes.
- Provide paper and writing tools for developing hand muscles as children record responses (in their own way) to science experiences.
- Observe to identify children who may need assistance with science activities because of less mature fine-motor control.

Developmental considerations
- Younger children are working on grasping, twisting, balancing, and other basic eye-hand skills. Provide easy-to-handle large objects and materials. (Activities involving eye-hand coordination require great effort and can be frustrating if too advanced.)
- Older children continue to enhance their fine-motor skills. Offer opportunities to work with tools that require more dexterity.

Scott Hewit, Ed.D., is an assistant professor at the Center for Teacher Education and Educational Services, State University of New York at Plattsburgh.

EXPLORING SCIENCE WITH SPECIAL-NEEDS CHILDREN

Hands-on science exploration is a wonderful experience for children with special needs. Experimenting with sensory materials such as water and sand can soothe as well as stimulate as children experience the kind of curiosity that leads to exciting discoveries. When an activity is truly open-ended and children can explore with materials on their own levels, in their own ways, then science is also a self-confidence builder.

SPECIAL NEEDS, SPECIAL CONSIDERATIONS

Children with special needs do need special consideration. Because they may not be able to fully explore with one or more senses or learn at the same pace as others, they may need more guidance to get the most from science investigations. Here are general ways to assist.

■ *Help children become familiar with science materials.* Children with handicapping conditions don't always use materials spontaneously. They will need lots of exposure to science tools and materials, and lots of time to see what each is for or can do. Some children may not recognize the properties of a material simply by handling it. Point out some of the properties to encourage purposeful exploration.

■ *To help children use materials independently, make sure they're comfortable exploring.* For example, when planting seeds, a child may need help spooning soil into a cup. Use the least amount of direction necessary. Provide the child with a set of materials and ask him or her to do the task with you. (If necessary, move the child's hands through the task.) Then offer less and less help to encourage the child to investigate more independently.

■ *Encourage cooperative experimenting.* Depending on a child's ability to work with others, invite her to explore with another child or a small group. Guide nonhandicapped children to accommodate the special needs of their peer. Remind them to speak directly to a hearing-impaired child; work on the level — floor or table — that's comfortable for a physically impaired child; describe what they are doing, calling objects by name, so that a visually impaired peer can join in; and accept a delayed child's participation, even when it doesn't mirror their own.

■ *Help children become aware of discoveries through exploration.* Focus the child by describing her actions. "You poured out all the water. Look, your cup is empty. Where is the water now?" Monitor activities to be sure they are novel enough to be interesting but not beyond the child's abilities.

■ *Reinforce science discoveries in other areas.* After experimenting with temperature, for example, draw a child's attention to warm and cold in other settings, such as foods at lunch and water when washing hands.

■ *Look for ways to boost each child's self-esteem.* Science can help children feel competent and successful. Children lacking muscle control, for example, gain confidence through activities, such as water play, that don't require precise movements. One approach to boosting self-esteem is to give a child a special job. For example, a visually impaired child might check whether the ice cubes have melted. A hearing-impaired child might use a keen sense of sight to watch for signs of insect life in soil. Praise a child as she masters a task: "You filled this whole dish with sand. That was hard to do!"

HELP FOR SPECIFIC HANDICAPS

Naturally, a child's specific handicapping condition impacts how he or she interacts with materials, tools, and other children in doing science activities. The tips below are general. Consult family members and therapists for guidance when working with individual children.

■ **Children with visual impairments** — Encourage the child to use other senses to compensate for the lost sight. Urge the child to *hold* objects, to *smell* and *taste* safe substances, and to *listen* for sounds things make. Draw the child's attention to shapes, sizes, weights, temperatures, and textures. Describe colors or patterns he or she cannot see.

To help the child make use of what sight she has, be sure the science area is well lit. Light should be nonglaring and evenly distributed. White butcher paper on tables and solid-colored materials and containers are easier to see.

■ **Children with hearing impairments** — While they observe and conduct experiments, hearing impaired children may miss explanations and discussions that help them fully understand and enjoy a science activity. When you share information — especially safety rules — use visual aids and demonstrations. Talk at a normal speed and volume at a distance that's best for the child to hear. During exploratory activities, talk with the child and ask questions to check understanding.

■ **Children with physical handicaps** — Touch-sensitive children are often wary of handling new or highly sensory materials, which abound in the science center. Offer gradual exposure. Describe the texture, then encourage the child to try a quick touch or a gentle stroke, working up to prolonged handling.

Help the child find a position that allows for greatest movement, such as on the floor over a bolster, sitting in a wheelchair, or secured to a chair. As needed, rearrange materials or equipment, such as putting them on portable trays.

Wrap hand tools with heavy tape to increase their width and make them easier to handle. Attach tools to a table with string so the child can retrieve them independently if they fall.

■ **Mentally retarded children** — Young retarded children operate at a sensory-motor level. They can't comprehend abstract concepts and learn best by focusing on the properties of objects or materials. Let the child work at a level he or she is comfortable with, while encouraging him to try new tasks he's capable of doing. Retarded children often shy away from what's new, preferring what's familiar.

When the child works with a group, be sure to modify your expectations. If a small group is comparing objects by weight, for example, this child may recognize only the greatest differences.

■ **Children with behavior disturbances** — Behaviors such as aggressiveness, withdrawal, or hyperactivity can interfere with children's abilities to interact with others and get the most from science experiences. Children who exhibit aggressive behavior, for example, probably find it difficult to share, and so need plenty of materials to choose from and space to work in. Praise them for working well alone and/or with others.

Children who act withdrawn may need to observe an activity before trying it on their own. Look for comfortable ways for them to interact with others, such as filling containers with water for a group experiment.

Children who exhibit hyperactivity do best with short activities so they can feel a sense of closure before trying something new. As with aggressive behavior, watch for signs of restlessness. Take steps before a child loses control.

Merle Karnes, Ed.D., is professor of special education at the University of Illinois at Urbana.

SETTING UP
FOR SCIENCE

A science center is one of many places in your room where science explorations occur. The water table and the sandbox are also science areas. So is a windowsill where plants are growing. Yet, despite the integrated nature of science, you need a special place to set up discovery activities and display charts, graphs, and collections, as well as a place to store science-oriented materials for easy access. By designating a special area for science investigations, you communicate to children and families that hands-on exploratory science is an important part of your program.

The location, size, and arrangement of furniture and materials in your science center all impact how children use it and how frequently they participate. As you think about setting up or rearranging your science center, use the guidelines and the suggested diagram in this section to help you create a physical space that encourages the excitement and challenge you want children to experience as they "do" science.

LOCATING AND FURNISHING THE AREA

First step: Choose a space. Ideally, you'll want to place the area close to water and sand areas, and near a water source. The squeals of delight that greet wondrous discoveries and the general need to share ideas, tools, and experiments mean this center can at times get noisy, so locate it accordingly. As you consider how much space to allot and how to furnish the area, remember to factor in the following.

What will you need in your setup?
■ *Storage space for adults* for materials not in use. If possible, use cupboards with doors so that materials are out of children's reach and out of sight.
■ *Child-sized storage space* that allows children to select and put away materials independently. Low, open shelves work best and can help separate this area from other parts of the room.
■ *Children's workspaces,* such as child-

sized tables and chairs; individual floor mats or rugs; trays to use on tables or the floor; and small round tables for four to six children that fit into odd spaces and encourage team exploration.

■ *Discovery-display spaces* for special activities. When arranged on trays, materials and equipment for specific science activities can be stored on top of low shelves, then moved to tables when children are ready to investigate. (See page 32 for tips on using tray setups.)

■ *Visual-display spaces* for charts, drawings, and other examples of children's work. Walls, bulletin boards, or the backs of shelf units are all good display areas.

How much space should you allow?

You know children need ample space to move around and be able to select activities with ease. Younger children, especially twos, need more open space because it's harder for them to maneuver to get something from a shelf. And children of all ages need plenty of elbow room when they work at tables. Many prefer standing at a table to sitting in a chair, and they're just as likely to spread out on the floor.

However, the dimensions of your science center will naturally depend on the total dimensions of your room. In a large setting, have fun creating a spacious area that offers a wide variety of activities. Provide lots of shelf space for materials and several tables at which children can work. In a smaller setting, you may be limited to one shelf unit and a small worktable. In a very small room, you may need to keep science materials in one section of a shelf unit housing other activities, like puzzles and games. Children's workspace may be a multipurpose table nearby.

But remember, even in a small space, a science center can still be active and inviting. What matters most is the kind of activities children engage in and providing enough of even a limited number of items so that more than one child can enjoy the activity. To accommodate

their need for space, decide how many children can comfortably use the center at one time.

What arrangements are best for different kinds of activities?

Some science activities are by nature more active, noisy, and messy than others. In a large center, consider placing the quieter table activities on one side and materials for more active exploration on another. In a smaller setting, keep more active or noisy explorations in your science center and display items that encourage quiet observation, such as an aquarium, in a quiet corner.

■ *Quiet activities* are best in a more protected area, perhaps close to a wall. These might include science books, magazines, and pictures displayed on a low shelf; materials for matching and sorting; and collections to observe, such as delicate seashells.

■ *Materials for active exploration* might be placed closer to the open side of your area, where they won't intrude on quiet activities and where they can be easily taken out of the center when more space is needed. Such materials might include balance scales, magnets, prisms, mirrors, and lenses.

■ *Messy activities* indoors are often located in their own special areas. For ease of management, water-play, planting, and cooking activities may occur near the sink, while sand play may be set up in a low-traffic area. There may be times, however, when you'll want to bring these activities into the science area for a special focus.

ORGANIZING AND MANAGING THE AREA

■ *Define individual workspaces.* Sharing space and materials is difficult for some children, and proximity to others may cause conflict. Use trays and floor mats to help define individual workspaces and materials.

■ *Promote independence.* Set up your science center so children can work with maximum independence. Materials should be within easy reach. Picture

strainers, sieves, rotary egg beaters, bowls, straws, spoons, basters, and eyedroppers
- plastic pails, buckets, and shovels
- clear plastic tubing
- boats and bath toys
- sponges, mops, and hand towels
- small whisk broom and dustpan

Recycle: clear plastic bottles with spray or squirt tops for water play; and packing pieces, cork, cardboard, foil, and waxed paper for floating and sinking experiments

Physical-Science Studies

(magnets, machines, heat, and light)
- magnets of various sizes, shapes, and strengths
- metal and non-metal objects
- wheels, gears, and pulleys
- tools/gadgets (especially tongs and tweezers for gripping/grasping)
- balance scale
- ramps, balls, and wheeled objects
- hot plate and cooking utensils
- pots, pans, cups, and bowls
- freezer and ice cubes
- indoor and outdoor thermometers
- magnifying and reducing lenses
- binoculars and kaleidoscopes
- prisms and plastic mirrors
- plastic flashlights

Recycle: colored cellophane and acetate for light experiments; metal juice lids; old appliances to take apart; and old kitchen utensils

As you pick up on children's interests and focus on other science topics, brainstorm lists like these to prepare your science center for true discovery learning.

labels on containers and shelves help children find and put away materials on their own. Displays should be at children's eye level.

■ *Provide clear choices and an adequate supply of materials.* Too many choices can be overwhelming. Begin with just a few materials. Later, when children know how to use the center, add more choices. Ideally, there should be enough materials so that two to four children can work on the same activity without having to share or wait for a turn. It's better to offer *more* of a limited number of materials than to present a great variety of materials with few duplicates. If storage space is a problem, keep extras in teacher storage.

■ *Avoid clutter.* Arrange materials neatly on open shelves. Leave enough space between materials to ensure visibility and easy access. Avoid stacking different kinds of materials. This leads to accidents when children try to pull the bottom items free.

■ *Think safety.* Materials not meant for

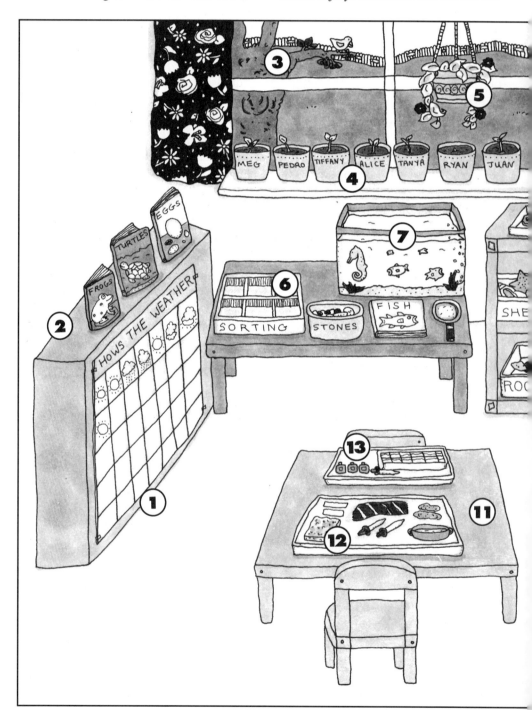

children's independent use need to be out of their sight and reach. Store special collections and materials that require supervision on high shelves. In the twos' room, there should be plenty of high shelf and counter space, not only to store materials not in use, but to provide space so that activities can be whisked away when necessary. (For more safety tips in the science center, turn to page 20.)

■ *Set rules, with children's help.* Children need to be clear about rules for using the space and materials. They should know how many children are permitted in the area at one time, and where and how materials may be used and cared for. Involve older children in making rules, and be sure everyone is clear on the reason for each.

■ *Demonstrate care.* Keep materials in good repair. Check that they're arranged neatly where they belong before each day begins. If you demonstrate care for the science center, children will, too.

for more safety tips in the science center, turn to page 20.

A SUPER SETUP

The illustration at left shows a science center. The numbers in the illustration correlate with the suggestions below. Please refer to "Setting Up for Science," pages 28-32, for more detailed guidelines.

1. Weather chart on back of shelf divider

2. Science books displayed on top of shelf

3. Window

4. Seedlings in paper cups or recycled cans (labeled with children's names)

5. Hanging plant

6. Sorting tray with dish of stones next to it

7. Aquarium with a magnifying glass for close viewing

8. Low shelf with science trays of: nuts and bolts; a balance scale; shells; pine cones; feathers (pushed into a plastic-foam block); rocks; and magnets

9. Posters and animal pictures on back of shelf divider

10. Sign-up system

11. Small table and two chairs

12. Tray with eyedroppers, small dish of water, sponge, fabric, paper, and foil samples

13. Tray with ice-cube tray full of water, food-coloring bottles, and an eyedropper

14. Sand/water table with clean sand in it

15. Shelf with sand toys — plastic bottles, funnels, small animals, small cars, popsicle sticks, etc.

16. Sink

ORGANIZING TIP:
TRY TRAY SETUPS

Setting up trays that hold materials and equipment for individual investigations helps structure science activities and encourage creative exploration and independent use. Generally, you'll want to set up each tray with enough materials for one child. For example, a tray might hold a container of pinecones, a pine branch with needles and pinecones attached, and a magnifying glass. Another might sport a large magnet, with an assortment of metal and non-metal objects to test. A third might feature a balance scale and metal washers of different weights.

Whether a child carries the tray from its place on the shelf or sits at a table where the tray is displayed, the materials are now the child's to work with and the tray defines his or her workspace. By preparing tray setups so that several children can try the same activity at once, you cut down on waiting time and children can still compare their discoveries, trading ideas and explanations.

Tray setups also make cleanup easier. Everything goes back on the tray, and the tray goes back to its place on table or shelf!

KEEP YOUR SCIENCE CENTER EXCITING

A science center has a lot to compete with in an early childhood setting. Blocks, art, and pretend play all offer wonderful possibilities for action and individual expression. Children may overlook the science center if the activities there seem dull or too adult-directed. These tips will help keep your science center alive!

■ *Encourage interaction with materials.* To capture children's attention, science explorations should encourage active participation and interaction with materials. As you know, children need to *do*, and the most effective science setups suggest they can. For example, a mounted collection of shells won't sustain interest for long. To make this display more interactive, add containers of loose shells and perhaps a simple shell identification book or chart to encourage matching and classifying activities.

■ *Evaluate each activity's success.* Define your goals for each activity. What would you like children to experience? As you observe, ask yourself: Is the activity fostering creative exploration? Are the materials being used in the ways you hoped or expected? Is the setup helping or hindering the discovery process?

Note the materials children select and how they use them. Are there some activities children ignore? Perhaps they need to be displayed where they can be seen more easily or arranged in a more appealing way. You might spark new interest by changing the materials only slightly. For example, interest in your shell collection might be revived by adding a magnifying lens.

■ *Rotate activities.* Are there materials and activities that were popular but now are rarely used? Even a fascinating wasps' nest or a fun activity with magnets will eventually lose its appeal. Observe to determine when children are becoming bored with an activity, then put it away. In a few months, children will have grown and changed and may now use the same materials in very different ways.

INTEGRATING SCIENCE WITH OTHER KINDS OF PLAY

A rich science program encompasses activities beyond the science center. Integrating science skills, concepts, and discoveries into other kinds of play helps children see science as an exciting all-day, everyday activity, indoors and out. Here are ways to integrate as children play in the different settings.

■ *Block corner* — Experiment with balance and leverage, and explore simple machines such as ramps, wheels, and pulleys.

■ *Art area* — Mix colors; explore and compare properties of different materials used in collage and construction art; and compare the consistencies and effectiveness of different pastes and glues.

■ *Water table* — Explore bubbles, moving water, pressure and suction, and floating and sinking.

■ *Sand area* — Experiment with wet and dry sand, use toy construction machines, and sort shells and stones.

■ *Cooking center* — Observe how water and heat change materials; "dissect" fruits and vegetables to find the seeds inside; and note how ingredients change at different stages.

■ *Dramatic-play area* — Pick up on children's interests, and encourage science-related play themes, such as a "medical center" with books, charts, and X-rays.

■ *Quiet corner* — Set up an aquarium or terrarium, or house your group pet here for quiet observation. Display books related to science themes for children to enjoy independently.

■ *Outdoors* — Experiment with the properties of pendulums (swings), levers (seesaw), and ramps (slide) on the playground; dig in sand and soil; observe animals, insects, and plant life; investigate shadows; watch clouds; and play with the wind. Just about anything children do outdoors will have a science dimension!

SHARING THE WONDER OF SCIENCE WITH FAMILIES

As you observe the delight children experience and the pride they feel as they create, manipulate, and discover in the science center, of course you'll want to share that with their families. And more, you'll want families to participate in the joy of science through discovery activities at home. If you're concerned you may meet with a "Science? Not me!" response, remember that, for some adults, "science" conjures up images of dull lectures about remote topics and classes where knowing the facts was more important than discovering the possibilities. You can help parents and other family members understand where science education is today and overcome their negative science stereotypes.

Many Ways to Communicate

To demonstrate young children's enthusiasm for science, invite families to witness it firsthand. They can help supervise a trip to a children's exhibit at a science museum, or help set up displays showing children's dictated observations of a pet or conclusions about why something happened during an experiment. Or ask family members to join in the fun in the science center. Share materials with families that support your philosophy. The send-home letter on page 34 is one way to communicate these important ideas. See the list at right for others.

As you discuss your science program in casual conversations, activities or letters, or in hands-on workshops, remember the following points and you will enhance your families' comfort with and understanding of science.

■ **Help family members recognize the value of concrete activities**. Explain how hands-on explorations contribute to science learning now and in later years.

■ **Let parents know how important they are to their child's learning.** Point out that when parents and family members show interest in observing and exploring, they send important messages to their children about the value and joy of those activities.

■ **Reassure parents that they don't need to know a lot of science themselves.** Emphasize the value of saying, "Let's find out together." Explain why it's less important for children to learn facts than to learn how to find out by observing and experimenting on their own.

■ **Help parents recognize that children are natural scientists**. Innate curiosity leads to exciting discoveries. Help family members find ways to support children as they explore and experiment.

■ **Point out that science experiences are all around us.** When they take their children on nature walks, dig in the sand or soil, or watch a plant grow together, families are helping their children develop science concepts and skills.

■ **Help adults ask questions that stimulate creativity.** Discuss the importance of questions that encourage children to test and explore, and allow for many possible answers or solutions.

SHARING THIS BOOK WITH FAMILIES

Along with the letter to families on the next page, feel free to duplicate and share the following sections of *Learning Through Play: Science*.

Learning and Growing Through Science Developmental Chart
(pages 22-25)
Activity Plans: Twos
(pages 38-47)
Activity Plans: Threes
(pages 48-57)
Activity Plans: Fours
(pages 58-67)
Activity Plans: Fives
(pages 68-77)

Use these ready-to-go pages to support families with information and ideas as they look to enhance their young child's sense of wonder and joy of discovery.

DISCOVERING SCIENCE TOGETHER AT HOME

Dear Family,

As you know, from the moment they're born, children explore with their fingers and mouths, investigating the amazing things around them, as well as their own place in a mysterious, marvelous world. From birth, children are natural scientists, and there are many ways you can help your young scientist grow. Observe. Listen to your child's questions and comments. Find out what your child is interested in and plan experiences that build on those interests. Talk about the fascinating discoveries your child is making about the world.

Here are some additional points to keep in mind as you explore together.

■ **You don't have to know all the answers.** Children often want to know everything, and a barrage of questions can be exhausting. Instead of trying to have all the answers, respond with, "Let's find out." Then head to the children's library, or ask a neighbor, a merchant, a doctor, or a dentist. Showing your child *how* to find more information and helping him or her understand that no one has to know everything is far more valuable in the long run!

■ **Help your child become a good observer.** Observing is more than just seeing. It involves using all the senses. Together, look, listen, taste, touch, and smell the world around you. Encourage your child to be aware of changes — in weather patterns, in the seasons, in pets, and in his or her own self.

■ **Experiment together.** Children often ask, "What would happen if ... ?" or "Why?" When it's safe and reasonable, you might answer, "That's a good question. Let's experiment to find out." Encourage your child to predict what might happen, and then let your child do as much of the experimenting as possible.

■ **Listen to your child's ideas and opinions.** When your child explains why something happened, it shows he or she is thinking. Remember, at this age being correct is not what's important. What is important is that your child is forming ideas, making predictions, and drawing conclusions on his or her own. After all, scientists need to think and rethink ideas, too!

■ **Help your child grow up loving science.** Share your own curiosity and ideas. Play, explore, and learn together. Model respect for all living things to help your child see that everyone and everything has a place in the world.

Happy Discovering!

_____

Teacher

ACTIVITY PLANS
FOR TWOS, THREES, FOURS, AND FIVES

USING THE
ACTIVITY PLANS

You know that many of the most successful science experiences with young children are not "planned." They start with a wondrous discovery — an insect never seen before, a bird nesting in a playground tree, or an "accident" that demonstrates how some objects sink while others float. From this spontaneous beginning, science exploration quickly develops. Children's natural curiosity takes over as they question and contemplate the meaning of what they observe. And through hands-on experiments, they get a good start at understanding how their world works.

The 40 child-centered plans that follow, designed for children ages two to five, are not meant to *replace* these serendipitous experiences. Rather, they're designed to *enhance* them. The activity themes — plants, animals, weather, the senses, magnets, water, shadows, simple machines — are the very subjects children are most likely to be intrigued by naturally. What the plans offer is help in structuring science activities that are appropriate to their developmental abilities and interests.

So on a day when it's raining outside, pull out an activity plan on rain or water. Or when it's sunny out and impromptu games of shadow tag are happening on the playground, look for an activity that will extend children's enjoyment into an understanding of how shadows are made and how they change throughout the day. In other words, turn to these plans when you see sparks of interest in a topic that, with help, will become an opportunity for real science excitement and learning.

UNDERSTANDING YOUR ROLE

More than many other parts of your program, science requires your active involvement. Children need time to explore, experiment, and solve problems on their own, but they also need you as a resource — not to answer all their questions, but to support and guide them through the process of testing their ideas and finding their own explanations.

The activity plans offer both you and your children the best in science exploration. Each plan is child-centered and designed to encourage hands-on involvement through simple experiments that the *children*, not you, will do. Yet the plans also provide you with help in fulfilling your role as a resource. You'll find open-ended questions to pique and extend children's ideas, as well as books that complement each activity. You can be confident that you're giving children plenty of time and space to make their own discoveries, while ensuring that their science experiences are rewarding and fun!

GETTING THE MOST FROM THE ACTIVITY PLANS

While the plans have been written and designed for children ages two to five, you know that these ages represent a wide range of developmental levels. You may find that certain plans need to be adapted to meet the particular needs and interests of your group. As you tune into your children's developmental levels, you can look for ways to enhance their interests and experiences with appropriate activities. The format is simple and easy to follow. Each plan includes most of these sections:

■ *Aim*: The value of the activity is outlined through a listing of the key science process skills, such as observing, classifying, and predicting, that will be tapped.

■ *Group size*: Suggested group size is the optimum number of children to involve at one time. Naturally, you can adjust this number to meet your needs.

■ *Materials*: Basic supplies from your science center or special items to gather are suggested here.

■ *In Advance*: This is an occasional heading found in some plans. It often suggests materials to prepare or arrangements to make before introducing an activity to children.

■ *Getting Ready*: Here you'll find ways to introduce the theme to a large

group at circle time or to a small group in the science center. Open-ended questions help children think about a topic. Brainstorming ideas, creating experience charts, taking a nature walk to observe or gather materials, or reading recommended stories are other ways to encourage involvement.

■ *Begin*: Now your young scientists truly take over! Suggestions for introducing the materials and for helping children get started are included with each plan. As well, there are open-ended questions to stimulate children's thinking and extend their explorations. Some activities also feature extension ideas to further enhance an experience.

■ *Remember*: This section offers developmental considerations to keep in mind. There may also be safety or health reminders or suggested ways to relate other skills and concepts to the activity, such as through art or writing.

■ *Books*: The books listed at the bottom of each page have been carefully selected to reinforce the science theme. They can be shared before or after the activity, whenever they seem to fit in best for you and the children, and they can also be displayed for children to explore at their leisure.

SHARING THE PLANS WITH OTHERS

To get the most from the activity plans, make them available to assistant teachers, to aides and volunteers, and to family members. (You have permission to duplicate all activity pages for educational use.)

When you share these plans, you communicate your philosophy of child-centered learning to others. By offering these tips on how to present hands-on activities, you help other adults to recognize the potential of science to both fascinate children and to help children feel more secure as they begin to grasp the workings of their highly complex world.

USING THE ACTIVITY INDEX

The index on pages 78-79 lists each activity plan, along with the developmental areas and science process skills it enhances. Use the index to:

■ determine the full range of skills and concepts covered in the plans

■ highlight specific skills or developmental areas a plan reinforces when talking with family members

■ identify and locate an activity that reinforces a particular science process skill on which you want to focus

■ assist you in finding activities that complement your group's present interests.

SCIENCE

Invite your twos to explore the wonders of light!

FUN WITH FLASHLIGHTS

Aim: Children will be introduced to properties of light as they explore with flashlights.
Group size: Whole group.
Materials: Flashlights, colored cellophane, a record or tape player, and records or tapes.

GETTING READY

Bring a flashlight to circle time. Pass it around so children can examine it, then ask who knows what this object is called. Turn the light on and off as a clue. When you've identified the flashlight, ask, "Have you ever seen someone at home use a flashlight? Can you show me how they used it?"

Invite children to take turns shining the flashlight. Challenge them to move the light beam slowly, then quickly, and to shine the light on the floor, ceiling, and walls. Then try these different activities with flashlights.

BEGIN

Flashlight Peek-a-Boo

Have children sit with their backs to you. Dim the room lights. Tell children that a little light beam is hiding and they must find it. Shine the flashlight around the room. Twos will get right into the fun of pointing to the beam when they spot it.

Colorful Lights

Tape colored cellophane over the lighted end of several flashlights. Shine the lights, and encourage twos to identify the colors of light they see. Let children manipulate the flashlights, seeing how objects in the room, even their own hair and skin, change color when the light shines on them.

Flashlight Follow-the-Leader

Invite twos to play follow-the-leader — with the light beam in the lead! Play a record or tape, then move the beam along the floor in time to the music. Children follow the light, moving quickly or slowly as it moves.

Sing a Song of Flashlights

Enjoy this song together. Encourage twos to extend an arm and fist to pantomime a flashlight.

Flashlight, flashlight
I shine it all around.
First on the ceiling (Point up to the ceiling.)
Then on the ground! (Point down to the floor.)

Remember

▪ Be sure to supervise twos carefully when using flashlights. Do the activity with small groups if you feel you can't adequately watch the whole group.
▪ A flashlight can be calming for some children. Tape posters of quiet scenes to the ceiling. At naptime, lie with restless children and shine the flashlight on the pictures as soft music plays in the background.

BOOKS

| Keep the lights dimmed as you read these sleepytime books. | ▪ *All the Pretty Horses* by Susan Jeffers (Scholastic) | ▪ *Close Your Eyes* by Jean Marzollo (Dial Books) | ▪ *Dr. Seuss' Sleep Book* by Dr. Seuss (Random House) |

ACTIVITY PLAN
READY-TO-USE TEACHING IDEAS FOR TWOS

SCIENCE

Indoors or out, twos can have fun with rain and snow.

RAIN AND SNOW ADVENTURES

Aim: Children will use observation skills as they enjoy the rain (and/or snow) inside and outside.

Group size: Two or three children (inside); whole group (with assistance) outside.

Materials: Plastic pan and assorted containers for pouring and dipping water or snow, plastic cloth, and waterproof smocks.

In Advance: Early in the day, place a pan outside to catch rainwater, or scoop up a pan of clean snow to bring indoors later.

GETTING READY

On a rainy or snowy day, gather children to talk about what they like to do on rainy or snowy days. Give them time to respond with ideas. If it's raining or snowing hard, plan all your activities for inside. If it's coming down lightly, suggest a walk outside to explore in the rain or snow. Be sure to dress children warmly. Try some of the children's ideas, and these.

BEGIN

Indoor Explorations

Weather Watch — Sit by the window with a few children at a time to watch the rain or snow. Ask, "Can you hear the rain (or snow)? What does it sound like?" Talk about how you can tell it's raining. (Puddles, people using umbrellas, things look wet, etc.) Ask children to tell what things they see that are getting wet or covered with snow.

Sing a Song — Sing along as you watch the rain or snow. This song is to the tune of "The Farmer in the Dell."

The rain is falling down,
The rain is falling down,
Heigh-ho, the merry-oh,
The rain is falling down.

Water and Snow Play — Place the pan of water or snow and assorted containers for dipping and pouring on a table protected by a plastic cloth. As twos explore, ask, "How does the water feel? What do you do with water?" Describe their actions: "Chad is pouring the rainwater into the funnel." Do the same with snow play: "Tamar has a handful of snow. How does it feel?" Draw children's attention to melting snow. "Look, the snow is melting. It turns to water when it gets warm."

Outdoor Explorations

Encourage children to use all of their senses on your rain or snow walk. Ask, "Can you see the rain (snow)? Hold out your hand. How does it feel? Listen. What do you hear?" Model words that describe these sensory experiences: "The rain feels warm and wet." "The snow is cold and ticklish on my nose." "I hear splish-splash when we walk through a rain puddle!"

Remember

■ Even with proper outerwear, twos can still get wet on an outside walk and will need a change of clothing. To prepare for these kinds of spontaneous activities, ask families to send extra clothing to keep at school.

BOOKS

Share these wet-weather books with twos.

■ *Rain* by Robert Kalan (Greenwillow Books)

■ *The Snow* by John Burningham (Thomas Y. Crowell)

■ *The Snowy Day* by Ezra Jack Keats (Viking Penguin)

SCIENCE

What happens when twos use a tube as a ramp?

FUN WITH BALLS AND CARDBOARD TUBES!

Aim: Children will experiment with cause and effect as they use a simple machine, an inclined plane, to propel balls of different sizes.

Group size: Four or five children.

Materials: Cardboard tubes, such as gift-wrap or mailing tubes; several balls that can roll through the tubes, such as tennis, golf, and small rubber and plastic-foam balls; material scraps; a grocery box; and large, lightweight blocks.

GETTING READY

Gather children in a circle. Take turns rolling a ball back and forth among you. Then invite twos to help you find some new ways to roll balls so that they go very fast.

BEGIN

Ramp and Roll

Place a cardboard tube on the floor and elevate one end on a box, chair, or large block. Show children how to place a ball in the top of the tube and watch it roll out of the bottom! Then invite twos to try it with the different balls you have gathered. If possible, provide several tubes elevated at different levels with which to experiment. Watch as children use problem-solving skills to decide which size balls work best with which tubes.

Where's the Ball?

Use a square of material to cover one end of a tube. Let the ball roll down the tube. Then ask, "Where is the ball? Why didn't it come out?" Give children plenty of time to examine the tube and test it themselves to try to figure out why the ball stopped coming out.

Knock It Down!

Invite twos to build a tower with lightweight plastic blocks. Then help them position a tube so that the ball will roll out and knock over the blocks. Ask, "What makes the blocks fall over?" Help children experiment with the incline of the tube to see how to make the balls roll faster and knock over the blocks more spectacularly.

Remember

▪ Twos, at first, will be most excited by the balls. Give them time to hold, manipulate, and play with the balls before bringing out the tubes.

▪ Provide lots of balls of different sizes. To avoid skirmishes, plan for at least one ball for each child.

▪ Cardboard tubes will not hold up long with this kind of workout. Have extras on hand to replace those that get bent or torn.

BOOKS

Here are more books with good science ideas for younger children.

▪ *Infant/Toddler: Introducing Your Child to the Joy of Learning* by Earladeen Badger (McGraw-Hill)

▪ *Learning Games for the First Three Years* by J. Lewis and Isabelle Sparling (Berkley Publishing)

▪ *Things to Do with Toddlers and Twos* by Karen Miller (Telshare)

SCIENCE

Twos discover the world of science through their senses. Let's start out with touch.

INDOOR/OUTDOOR FEELY FUN!

Aim: Children will use observation skills as they investigate outdoor and indoor environments for shapes, colors, and textures.
Group size: Three or four children.
Materials: Three plastic pans; clean, dry sand; plastic-foam peanuts; clean aquarium gravel; assorted containers for digging, scooping, and pouring; and one glove for each child.

GETTING READY

Gather twos to focus on hands. Encourage them to wiggle their fingers and show how hands can hold and grasp. Talk about how hands help us eat, carry things, and hug friends. Count together to find out how many hands and how many fingers each child has.

BEGIN

Indoor Investigations

Take a walk around your room. Touch the table, chairs, rug, floors, walls, etc. Open the windows and feel the air outside. Talk about the size, color, and texture of the objects children are touching: "The red rug is rough and scratchy." Encourage children to tell which objects feel smooth and which feel rough.

As you continue your touch walk, sing this song together. It's to the tune of "Merrily We Roll Along."

Touch, touch, touch the floor,
Touch the floor together.
Touch, touch, touch the floor,
It feels so smooth and hard!

Replace "floor" with rug, window, walls, etc., and "smooth and hard" with words describing these other parts of the room.

Feely Finger Fun

Fill each of three plastic pans with sand, plastic-foam peanuts, and aquarium gravel. Provide containers for children to experiment with mixing, pouring, scooping, and stirring each type of material. Talk about how each item feels as children work. "This gravel feels bumpy. You can squish these peanuts with your fingers."

Outdoor Investigations

Take a walk outside to look for different textures. Feel the grass, flower petals, tree bark, dirt, cement pavement, and a car parked safely nearby. Ask, "Who can touch something that's

soft? That's hard? That's smooth?"

Add a twist to the feely fun. After children have touched each outdoor object with a bare hand, cover one hand with a glove. Ask, "How does the tree feel now?" Touch with other body parts, too, such as arms, elbows, legs, etc.

Remember

■ Twos will have favorite textures that they like to feel and that may be soothing for them. Place items with those textures in a cardboard box. Let children remove these items at leisure, especially at times when a stroke of a furry stuffed friend or a velvety shawl may be comforting.

BOOKS

| Here are books to read about touch and hands. | ■ *I Touch* by Helen Oxenbury (Walker) | ■ *My Hands Can* by Jean Holzenthaler (E.P. Dutton) | ■ *Sticky Stanley* by Thomas Crawford (Troll) |

SCIENCE

Continue the sensory exploration with a favorite experience — tasting and eating!

JOIN THE TASTING PARTY!

Aim: Children will use their sense of taste and language skills to identify and describe different foods.

Group size: Three or four children.

Materials: Small bowls or paper plates; spoons and napkins; and foods that have distinct sweet, sour, and salty tastes. Possible sweet foods include applesauce, grapes, bananas, or fruit breads or muffins; possible sour foods include lemon and lime wedges and sour pickles; possible salty foods include pretzels and other salted snacks.

In Advance: Choose one or two foods from each category. Cut the foods into bite-sized pieces that can be easily picked up with fingers and spoons, and arrange them on plates or in bowls. Set a place for each toddler at a table, and bring out the food.

GETTING READY

Invite twos to the table and point to each food you have arranged there. Ask, "Can anyone tell me what kind of food this is? Has anyone ever tasted it before?" Talk about how different kinds of foods have different tastes.

BEGIN

Help each child take a small amount of each kind of food. As children sample, talk about what they are eating: "Marvin, do you like those pretzels? They're salty, aren't they?" "Nadine, does that pickle squirt when you bite it? Does it taste sour?"

Ask children which foods they like most. Help them use the words *sweet*, *sour*, and *salty* in describing the foods. Extend twos' language skills by helping them find other words that describe the foods they tasted, such as *chewy*, *crunchy*, *squishy*, *wet*, and *soft*.

As you enjoy different snacks each day, build on this activity by describing the foods as *sweet*, *sour*, or *salty*, while adding words that tell about their texture or appearance.

Remember

▪ Don't forget to wash everyone's hands before starting the activity.

▪ Twos have favorite foods and may want to eat only what is familiar. Some foods may not get tasted by anyone. Don't force the tasting. Let twos observe and listen as you taste and talk about the untried items.

▪ Some twos will do more eating than speaking. Offer a little at a time so they don't stuff themselves.

▪ Keep wet paper towels and a wastebasket handy for easy cleanup. Twos can wash their own faces and hands and clear their space at the table.

BOOKS

Look for these books for more ideas on cooking and eating fun with young children.

▪ *Creative Food Experiences for Children* by Mary Goodwin (Center for Science in the Public Interest)

▪ *Cup Cooking: Individual Child Portion Picture Recipes* by Barbara Johnson and Betty Plemons (Gryphon House)

▪ *The Lucky Cookbook for Boys and Girls* by Eva Moore Talwaldis (Scholastic)

SCIENCE

Have fun with the wind on a windy day.

WATCH THE WIND

Aim: Children will observe and experiment with things that move in the wind.

Group size: Whole group.

Materials: Tape, paper streamers, and/or newspaper strips of different lengths; bubble solution and wands; and a notebook and marker.

GETTING READY

On a windy day, gather children at a window where everyone can see clearly outside. Comment on the effects of the wind. Ask, "What can you see moving outside? What might make the trees and papers move? Can the wind make things move?" Now invite children to go with you on a walk outside to watch the wind. Bring along a notebook and marker for recording the children's observations.

BEGIN

As you walk, talk about the way the wind whips and moves objects: "Janine, I see you caught a green leaf that was blowing in the wind." "Denny, look at the way the wind makes your shirt ripple." As children respond to effects of the wind, write down their comments to share back inside.

Breezy Bubbles and Streamers

After your walk or on another windy day, give each child a streamer to hold as it blows in the wind. Comment on the way the streamers move. Do they ripple like waves in the wind? Do they stand out almost straight? Help children tape their streamers to a nearby pole or tree and watch them move in the wind.

Now introduce the bubble solutions and wands. Children will love watching the bubbles they blow being carried away by the wind. Encourage children to see how far the wind takes the bubbles before they pop. Let them take turns blowing and chasing bubbles.

Say a Windy Chant

Add this chant to your windy-day activities. Ask twos to take turns naming something the wind blows.

> *The wind blows fast.*
> *The wind blows slow.*
> *What does the wind blow?*
> *Do you know?*

Remember

▪ Use your judgment in taking children out on a windy day. If it's cool, be sure they're dressed warmly, wearing hats to cover ears. A good breeze will make observation more interesting, but strong gusts may frighten children.

▪ Tape a few streamers to a tree that children can see from indoors. Invite twos to check the streamers daily for signs of wind.

▪ Look for other items to test in the wind, such as scarves, ribbons, and paper bags. Be sure to pick up your litter before returning to the room.

▪ For a related movement activity, play lilting music and ask twos to pretend to be a bubble or a tree being blown about by the wind.

BOOKS

Share these books on another object the wind likes to play with — a balloon.

▪ *Belinda's Balloon* by Emilie Boon (Alfred A. Knopf)

▪ *Lillie Goes to the Playground* by Jill Krementz (Random House)

▪ *My Balloon* by Catherine Chase (Dandelion)

SCIENCE

Your twos will love to make bird feeders and watch birds eat.

FOR THE BIRDS

Aim: Children will use observation skills as they watch birds' activities in their natural settings.

Group size: Whole group for the walk; three or four children for making bird treats.

Materials: Stale bread, peanut butter, and birdseed; cookie cutters; tongue depressors; and string or yarn.

In Advance: Prepare children for bird-watching by sharing the book *A Year of Birds* or a similar book on birds. Display pictures of birds in the science area. Encourage children to watch for birds in trees near the window and observe their activities. This activity will help build interest in making food for the birds. And knowing ahead of time where birds are often found near the school increases the likelihood of seeing birds — or signs of birds — on an outdoor walk.

GETTING READY

Bring your group together and suggest going for a walk to look for birds. Share pictures of things they should look for — feathers, nests, broken eggs, etc. During the walk, remind twos what they are searching for: "I see a bird's nest up in that tree. Does anyone see the birds who live in this tree?"

After your walk, review with children what they observed, then talk about what kinds of foods birds eat. Ask, "Who knows what birds eat?" Always give twos plenty of time to respond before prompting with more questions such as, "Do birds eat worms? Do they eat seeds?" Then invite interested children to take turns making a special meal for the birds near your school.

BEGIN

Place cookie cutters and stale bread on a table. Ask children to cut shapes from bread with the cookie cutters. Next, have them use tongue depressors to spread peanut butter on their shapes, then sprinkle on birdseed. Finally, thread a piece of yarn through each shape and hang outside on a tree near a window in your room.

It may take several days for birds to find this new source of food. It's hard for twos to wait. Keep watch yourself while involving the children in other activities such as observing a canary, parakeet, or other bird friend that might visit for a few days. When birds do start to feed outside, observe with twos and talk about the behaviors that they may notice but not have the words to describe.

Remember

▪ Twos are likely to think of peanut butter as people food. Schedule this activity for after a lunch or snack of peanut butter. Explain that children have had their food and now they'll make some for the birds.

▪ To avoid having birdseed all over the room, pour a thin layer in a shallow tray. Show twos how to press the peanut-butter bread into the seed, or how to hold the bread over the tray while sprinkling on the seed. Either way, what doesn't stick drops back onto the tray instead of the floor. Refill the tray as needed.

▪ Birds will come to count on a food source. Make fixing treats for them a regular activity, or hang up a standard feeder. The opportunities for ongoing observation of birds should be worth the expense.

BOOKS

Here are some books about birds and the outdoors.

▪ *A Year of Birds* by Ashley Wolff (Dodd, Mead and Company)

▪ *The Park* by Eric Hill (Random House)

▪ *Spring Days* by Harold Roth (Grosset & Dunlap)

SCIENCE

Even your youngest will enjoy experimenting by filling and emptying containers.

HOLDING THEIR OWN

Aim: Children will use observation, classification, and language skills as they experiment with containers to see which ones hold substances and which ones don't.

Group size: Two to four children.

Materials: One "exploration" (sand or water) table or several dishpans filled with sand or water; containers that can hold the substances, such as measuring cups, small plastic bowls, cups, spoons, and possibly sponges; containers that cannot hold sand or water, such as sieves, funnels, slotted spoons, etc.; a large towel or drop cloth; and waterproof smocks for water explorations.

GETTING READY

Invite a few children to join you at the sand or water table. Have a variety of containers on hand for children's exploration. Give them plenty of time to experiment with the containers, filling them with sand or water. Then talk about which containers will hold a substance and which will not. Help children to verbalize their observations. "Michael, you filled that big cup with sand. But Larry's funnel let the sand go right through, didn't it?" You might encourage children to experiment with other items they have not tried: "Consuelo, let's see how much water this strainer will hold."

BEGIN

Put the containers and utensils in a bag or bucket. Go around the table and invite each child to choose one and to experiment with it. Comment on children's actions and ask questions, as needed, to help them draw conclusions about the various items: "Cindy, it looks like you're having trouble keeping water in that sieve. Do you think it can hold water?"

Give other children a chance to see if they can make the sieve hold water. Once everyone is satisfied, put the sieve into a pile of items that will not hold water or sand. Do the same with the remaining containers and utensils, until all have been categorized as "good holders" or "bad holders."

If children begin to lose interest, encourage them to scout the room (especially the kitchen area) for more items they think will hold water or sand. Help them try out their items at the exploration table and place them in the proper pile.

Follow Up With Sharing

Help children find the words to tell you which container they like to use best and why. One child may prefer the sponge because it sucks up water. Another might like the bowl because it holds so much. A third might like the spoon because he or she can pick up just a little sand at a time.

Remember

▪ The focus is on whether the container will or will not hold water or sand. Don't try to compare the quantities the different containers hold or introduce other advanced concepts.

▪ Be prepared for sand or water to overflow onto the floor and onto children. Wear smocks and use a floor covering such as a large towel or drop cloth.

BOOKS

Here are more science resources with activities to do with very young children.

▪ *Bubbles, Rainbows, and Worms* by Sam Ed Brown (Gryphon House)

▪ *Rub-a Dub-Dub, Science in the Tub* by James Lewis (Meadowbrook Press)

▪ *Small Wonders: Hands-On Science Activities for Young Children* by Peggy K. Perdue (Scott, Foresman & Co.)

SCIENCE

Invite twos to observe the fascinating properties of magnets!

MAGNIFICENT MAGNETS

Aim: Children will use observation and classification skills as they explore the properties of magnets.

Group size: Four children.

Materials: Four large magnets; a box of assorted metallic and non-metallic objects such as metal, plastic, and wooden spoons; metal and plastic combs; a large metal washer or ring; a large rubber ring; small metal scissors; small plastic scissors; metal, wooden, and plastic knobs about two inches in diameter; cardboard, fabric, and magnetic strips; and small metal and plastic dishes.

GETTING READY

Invite several children to come to the table and see what you have in the box. Pull out the items and encourage children to name them. Give them plenty of time to examine the items and see and feel their differences. Then show children the magnets and let them examine those. Demonstrate how the magnets can pick up some of the objects.

BEGIN

Give each child a magnet and ask him or her to test to see which objects it can pick up. Ask, "Can your magnet pick up the white plastic spoon? Can it pick up the silver spoon?" As a child picks up something, comment on the action: "Sara's magnet picked up the metal ring. Nathan's magnet can pick up a metal spoon." Comment also on the objects children can't pick up: "Marta, your magnet won't pick up that plastic comb. Will it pick up the other comb?"

When interest in these objects wanes, encourage children to find other things in the room that stick to the magnet. Give them plenty of time to experiment with things in their environment.

Extend the experience by placing two magnets so that opposite poles touch. Ask two children to pull the magnets apart, and as they try, talk about how strong the magnets are. Separate the magnets, then let children explore trying to put the magnets together. Observe as they experience the sensations of having opposite poles attract or like poles repel.

Later, place the box of objects and the magnets in your science center so children can continue to make discoveries on their own.

Remember

- Be sure the objects you select are not a choking danger for twos. Small objects like safety pins, paper clips, and nuts and bolts are unsafe and unsuitable.

- Twos are too young to understand the whys of magnetic attraction. Keep the focus on discovering which objects will stick to a magnet. This early introduction will help lay a foundation of experience and curiosity about magnets that will benefit children years from now.
- Use two boxes to sort objects magnets can pick up and those they cannot. To help twos distinguish the boxes, put a picture of a magnet on the box of things magnets will pick up.

BOOKS

Continue the focus on interesting observations with these books.	■ *A Surprise for Your Eyes* by Arnold Shapiro (Price, Stern, Sloan)	■ *My Favorite Thing* by Gyo Fujikawa (J.B. Communications)	■ *What Do I See?* by Harriet Ziefert and Mavis Smith (Bantam)

SCIENCE

What fun to plant grass and watch it grow!

LET'S GROW GRASS

Aim: Children will use sensory and observation skills as they plant grass seeds and watch them grow.

Group size: Four children.

Materials: Grass seed, small paper cups, newspaper, potting soil, paper towels, spoons, water, and a small bowl.

In Advance: One week prior to the activity, plant a cup of grass. Fill a paper cup two-thirds full with potting soil. Sprinkle about half a teaspoon of grass seed on the soil, then add more dirt to cover the seeds and one teaspoon of water. Place on a sunny windowsill. The grass will sprout within days.

GETTING READY

Place newspaper on a table where children can prepare their seed cups. Put a bag of potting soil in the center of the table, along with cups, spoons, a dish of grass seed, and paper towels. Place a bowl of water on the table. Set out the cup of grass you've grown.

BEGIN

Invite small groups of interested children to come to the table to see your cup of grass. Encourage them to touch and smell the grass to see if they can tell what it is. If children cannot name it, tell them that you have grown grass, the kind that grows in the park or in their yards at home.

Next, show children the grass seed. Put several seeds in each child's hand. Encourage each to smell the seed and talk about its color and size. Identify the other items on the table. Let children examine the potting soil. Talk about how it feels and smells.

Now give each child a cup and spoon for planting grass seed. Have them fill their cups about two-thirds full with soil. Then have them scoop some seed from the bowl, sprinkle it onto the soil, then add more soil to cover the seeds.

Tell children that for seeds to grow, they need soil, water, and sunshine. Their seeds have soil, so now they need water. Supervise as they use their spoons to get water from the bowl to sprinkle into their cups. Ask children to help you find a sunny spot on a windowsill, and place the cups in the sunlight.

Set aside a certain time (such as right after nap or before lunch) every day for checking the cups together. When the grass sprouts, talk about how it changes as it grows. Take a walk outdoors to feel and smell grass.

Remember

▪ Do not overwater grass. A little goes a long way.

▪ For grass to look its best, it needs to be trimmed. Use scissors to cut your paper-cup "lawns."

▪ When the grass in the cups is growing well, children may like to transplant it in an area outside near their own homes or the school.

▪ Plant other seeds at other times of the year. Good choices include pumpkin seeds in fall and radish seeds in spring. For a dramatic effect, place a bean seed between a wet paper towel and a clear plastic cup. As the seed sprouts, the root, stems, and leaves will be easy to see. Don't get too involved in describing these plant parts. Twos will be fascinated just watching the changes in the plant as it grows.

BOOKS

Share more books about plants with your young gardeners.

▪ *The Carrot Seed* by Ruth Krauss (Harper & Row)

▪ *Let's Grow a Garden* by Gyo Fujikawa (Zokeisha Publications)

▪ *Wild Wild Sunflower Child Anna* by Nancy White Carlstrom (Macmillan)

SCIENCE

Threes often explore the world through their sense of touch, so make an activity of it.

CREATE A TEXTURE BOOK

Aim: Children will use observation, classification, language, and experimentation skills while exploring objects with different textures.

Group size: Three or four children.

Materials: A variety of different-textured materials such as cotton balls, scraps of velvet, aluminum foil, straw, sandpaper, burlap, dried leaves, etc.; large sheets of oaktag or construction paper; crayons, scissors, and a stapler; and old magazines.

GETTING READY

Set out a collection of different-textured items on a table. Be sure to include enough samples so that each child in the small group has textures to compare. You'll also want to be sure you have items of similar texture for classifying in groups.

Let children touch and explore the objects freely for a while. Then talk about the different textures. Ask, "What do your hands tell you about each of these?" Encourage children to feel the objects again. Help them find words to tell about each by modeling descriptive language: "Look, this one feels bumpy. Can you find another one that is bumpy?" Allow plenty of time for everyone to touch and comment.

BEGIN

Children will naturally begin to find objects that have the same texture — two furry objects, for example — or textures that have similar qualities. Help them group the like-textured items together. As they work, discuss the items. Ask, "Why do you think this one goes in this pile? How is it like these others?"

Some children may want to be "texture scientists." Give each an item to hold, then suggest the child search the room for another object that feels the same. The process of matching like textures helps children practice comparative thinking.

Make a Book

To save on materials, you may want to introduce this project only after all the children in the room have tried the activity above. Together, sort the textured scraps into similar piles. Then invite children to choose a pile and make a collage. Use each collage as a page, and collate the pages into a group texture book. Review it together, asking children to describe and compare the textures: "Jack says this page feels rough. Jack, what else is rough like these objects?" Display the book in your science area for children to enjoy on their own.

Remember

- As threes start this project, they may pick out only gross differentiations among the textures. Encourage children to sort in their own ways. As they work, point out more subtle differences, such as objects that are smooth but not shiny or bumpy but not rough.
- Extend the activity by creating a "texture cube." Invite children to paste texture scraps on the sides of a large cardboard box. Have them group materials so that one side has all rough objects, another all smooth, etc. Store the cube in your quiet corner. Feeling its textures can be a calming experience.

BOOKS

Share these books to help children understand more about texture.

- *Find Out by Touching* by Paul Showers (Thomas Y. Crowell)

- *My Bunny Feels Soft* by Charlotte Steiner (Alfred A. Knopf)

- *Pat the Bunny* by Dorothy Kunhardt (Golden Press)

SCIENCE

These sensory experiences all have the sweet smell of exciting discovery!

A NOSE WORKOUT

Aim: Children will use their sense of smell as they create and compare their own fragrance essences.

Group size: Three or four children.

Materials: Clear plastic cups, water pitchers, plastic spoons, and eyedroppers; ingredients with scents, such as vanilla extract, almond extract, mint extract, maple syrup, lemon juice, cinnamon, and other spices; foods with distinct smells, such as pickles, chocolate, ginger snaps, and peanut butter (on a cracker); brown paper lunch bags; a knife; napkins; chart paper and a marker; and men's or women's cologne.

In Advance: Prepare fragrance cups by filling each cup two-thirds with water. Add a few drops of *one* scent to each cup. Place the foods in separate bags.

GETTING READY

Introduce the focus on smell with a guessing game. Pass around one paper bag at a time and have children take turns smelling — but not looking at — its contents. Record their ideas on chart paper. Show the contents of each bag after each child has made a guess. When all of the foods have been identified, ask children how they guessed each item. Talk about how some foods have a distinctive smell. Ask, "Which part of our body do we use to smell things?" Finish by cutting the foods into small pieces for tasting.

BEGIN

Spritz a little cologne into the air. Position children so they can smell it, then ask them to describe the odor. Encourage children to share their own experiences playing with an adult's cologne or watching a family member use cologne or perfume.

Introduce the pre-made fragrance cups. Have each child smell the cups and try to guess the scents. Then invite children to use these scents to create their own colognes.

Give each child a few plastic cups and an eyedropper. Demonstrate how to use the eyedropper. Then have children carefully pour water from the pitcher into their cups. Encourage them to experiment by combining different mixtures until they have the smell they like best.

Pour the finished products into plastic bottles and label with each creator's name. With children's permission, place them in the dramatic-play area, where children can use the scents on themselves "when they go out" or on dolls.

Remember

▪ Threes are just beginning to develop a descriptive vocabulary. When asked to describe a smell, they may only tag it "good" or "bad." Expand their language skills by modeling more descriptive words like *sweet*, *spicy*, *flowery*, *sour*, etc.

▪ Some children will want to take their mixtures home instead of leaving them in the dramatic-play area. Be sure to respect their wishes.

▪ Extend the activity into a "smelly" finger-painting project by adding different extracts to finger paints or by setting out cinnamon or nutmeg that children can sprinkle onto a finished painting if they wish.

BOOKS

Cool down after your nose workout with these books that focus on the sense of smell.

▪ *Benny's Nose* by Mel Cebulash (Scholastic)

▪ *Detective Arthur on the Scent* by Mary J. Fulton (Golden Press)

▪ *Follow Your Nose* by Paul Showers (Thomas Y. Crowell)

SCIENCE

Search for "nature treasures" in the great outdoors around your preschool!

TAKE A NATURE WALK

Aim: Children will use observation, classification, prediction, and language skills as they look for natural items to combine in a collage.

Group size: Whole group for nature walk; four to six children at a time for making the collages.

Materials: Small paper bags, cardboard or plastic-foam grocery trays or paper plates, white glue, markers, construction paper, and chart paper.

GETTING READY

At circle time, talk about the discoveries you might make on a walk around your school. Ask, "What could we see on a walk outdoors? What kinds of things could we find?" On chart

paper, record children's predictions, such as leaves, rocks, grass, trees, etc.

BEGIN

Hand out bags to children, explaining that these are "treasure bags" for holding objects they'll gather on the walk. Discuss appropriate items to collect (rocks, leaves, grasses) and the kinds of things children shouldn't take (flowers from a garden, bird feathers, objects that might carry lice or disease, etc.).

Enjoy the walk outdoors. Use sensory words to describe the smells, sights, and sounds you encounter. Look for interesting rocks, seeds, leaves, plants, flowers, and nuts. Encourage children to collect objects to use in making nature collages. Talk about how the objects feel as they're gathered.

Back in the room, check your chart of predictions to help review the events of the walk. Talk about the things children saw and check them off. What else did children see that's not on the chart?

Make Nature Collages

Invite small groups of children to bring their treasure bags to a work table. Provide each child with a tray for holding the bag's contents. Encourage them to identify the objects, then sort them into piles by features. Which items are soft and which are hard? Which are big and which are little? Which are dark in color and which are light?

Set out white glue and paper plates or trays. Invite children to glue the objects onto plates or trays in any way they like. Display the collages.

Remember

▪ Avoid asking children to find "perfect" leaves, flowers, etc. Threes think of each object as a treasure. You help confirm that nature is beautiful in all forms, even imperfect ones, when you share in a child's delight with a worm-eaten leaf or broken twig.

▪ Let children create the collages in their own ways. Some may use every object they collected, while others will paste on a few and be done.

▪ Some children may not want to make a collage but will prefer to keep the objects loose, so they can examine them over and over. Be sure to respect their wishes.

▪ Have children wash their hands after the walk and after examining the objects they collect. Be sure children don't taste seeds, leaves, etc., as many types are poisonous.

BOOKS

Share these books with nature themes with threes.

▪ *A Day in the Woods* by R.M. Fisher (National Geographic)

▪ *All Upon a Stone* by J.C. George (Thomas Y. Crowell)

▪ *Once We Went on a Picnic* by Aileen Fisher (Thomas Y. Crowell)

SCIENCE

Threes will bubble with delight at this activity!

WHAT MAKES THE BEST BUBBLES?

Aim: Children will use problem-solving and language skills as they experiment with different ways to make bubbles.

Group size: Three or four children.

Materials: Bubble solution (see recipe below) and a bubble wand or pipe; a low flat pan, colanders, sieves, and berry baskets; six-pack plastic rings; egg beaters; plastic straws; food coloring; and white paper.

In Advance: Prepare the bubble solution following this recipe: Mix together 8 tablespoons liquid dish detergent, 1 quart water, and 1 tablespoon glycerine.

GETTING READY

Gather a small group. Use the bubble wand or pipe to demonstrate how to make bubbles. Give each child a turn at blowing bubbles. Then ask, "Have you ever seen bubbles in the bathtub or in the sink at home? Where else have you seen bubbles? What makes bubbles?" Give children plenty of time to respond with comments and ideas.

BEGIN

Invite children to investigate other kinds of objects that can be used to form bubbles. Fill a low pan or the water table with bubble solution. Provide a colander, sieve, or berry basket for children to experiment with, then stand back and let them find ways to use these items to make bubbles. Problem-solving skills will be at work as they figure out how to slowly lift the object so the soap

film doesn't break and how to blow on it or pull it through the air to make bubbles. Encourage children to compare the size of the bubbles the various objects make. Ask each to choose his or her favorite bubble maker.

Make It Colorful

Add a few drops of food coloring to the bubble solution, or make several pans with a different-colored solution in each. As children blow bubbles, ask them to tell you what colors they see.

Invite children to use the egg beater or straws to make mountains of bubbles in each pan. Pop the bubbles on sheets of white paper for abstract bubble pictures.

Remember

▪ Small bubble wands are hard for threes to use because of their limited fine-motor coordination. They'll really enjoy this activity because the larger objects are easier for them to manipulate.

▪ If children don't figure it out on their own, show them how to blow *gently* on the bubble solution to create more bubbles.

▪ Invite children to look around the room for other objects to use in making bubbles. At first they may try anything, but through trial and error they'll recognize that the object has to have a hole in it.

Activity plan based on an idea in *The New Kindergarten* by Jean Marzollo (Harper & Row).

BOOKS

Look for other great science activities for young children in these resources.

▪ *Bubbles, Rainbows, and Worms* by Sam Ed Brown (Gryphon House)

▪ *Guppies, Bubbles, and Vibrating Objects* by John McGavack and Donald La Salle (John Day)

▪ *Science Experiences for Young Children* by Viola Carmichael (Southern California EYC)

SCIENCE

"Laundry day" in the doll corner is a great time to explore concepts of wet and dry.

EXPERIMENTING WITH WET AND DRY

Aim: Children will observe and predict as they experiment with wet and dry.

Group size: Two or three children.

Materials: Water table or dishpans, water, gentle detergent, and waterproof smocks; clotheslines and pins; doll clothes; and a hair dryer and fan (optional).

GETTING READY

Introduce the doll clothing and talk about washing clothes. Ask, "Who washes clothes at your house? Do you ever help?" Give children plenty of time to share their experiences. Have each child choose a piece of doll clothing to wash. Then ask, "What will we need to wash these clothes? What will happen to the clothes when we put them in water?"

BEGIN

Help children put on their smocks, then invite them to help fill the water table or dishpans with water. Let them add the detergent to create suds.

Now it's time to wash the clothes! Threes will want plenty of time to enjoy this process. As they wash, ask questions that focus on differences between wet and dry. For example: "Do the wet clothes feel different? Do they look different? What makes them look and feel different?"

Rinse and wring out the clothes, then talk about how long it will take for the clothes to dry. Ask each child to make a prediction. Ask, "Which clothes do you think will dry the fastest? Which will take the longest to dry? Why?" Then ask children where in the room they think the clothes will dry the fastest. Hang up the clothesline in that place, and pin up the clothes according to the children's predictions (fastest to slowest). Check their progress periodically. Remember that the *process of thinking* is more important than the accuracy of the predictions.

If children do not choose a sunny spot for their clothesline, take them on a "temperature stroll" around the room. Ask children to tell you when they think they've found a good place in the room for drying clothes and why. Try all these different spots on subsequent washing days. Through experimenting, children should discover that the warmer, sunnier places are the best.

Try other drying methods, too. Bring in a hair dryer and fan to test, or wad up some wet clothes in a dark place and lay others flat in the sun. Ask children to predict which method will work best each time and why.

Remember

• There's a natural affinity between threes and water. They'll probably enjoy washing the doll clothes so much they'll want to do it again. On another day, let threes wash the furniture and furnishings in the dramatic-play area with sponges. Ask, "How does the furniture look different when it's wet? Which will take longer to dry, the dishes or the dish towel? Why?"

• Be sure to handle the hair dryer and fan yourself. Keep them out of children's reach.

BOOKS

Share these books about water, washing, and bathing.

• *Bathtime* by Alona Frankel (Barron's)

• *I Hate To Take a Bath* by Judi Barrett (Modern Promotions Publications)

• *Water Is Wet* by Sally Cartwright (Coward, McCann & Geoghegan)

SCIENCE

Watch threes "dig into" these science activities!

HAVE A MUD DAY!

Aim: Children will observe the properties of mud through hands-on experiences.

Group size: Whole group outside; three or four children inside.

Materials: Small trowels or sand shovels, containers (coffee cans, plastic tubs, and bowls), large spoons, watering cans, foil pie plates, construction paper, chart paper, and markers. Have children wear old clothes and boots. For disposable smocks, cut arm and neck holes in large plastic garbage bags.

GETTING READY

Take advantage of a good rainstorm to declare Mud Day. Gather children at circle time and ask, "What makes mud? Where does it come from?" Some children may be literal and say the rain makes mud. Others may make up amazing explanations. Accept all responses and record them on chart paper. Then ask, "What can we do with mud? How should we dress to play in the mud?"

BEGIN

Mud Fun Outside

Give children time to just explore. Talk about how the mud feels — cold? mushy? wet? Set out the shovels and containers and let children use them at will.

Set up situations where children can observe changes in the mud. For example, ask, "What will happen if we pour water into the mud?" Have an interested child try it, then ask, "How did the mud change?" Put a dish of mud in the sun and have children watch for change. Put a glob of mud on newspaper, then talk about how the paper absorbs the water from the mud. From these experiences, talk about what makes mud different from plain dirt (it has water mixed in it).

Make a mud person. Invite threes to shape the mud into balls for making a variation on a snowperson. If it's too wet, ask children for ideas of what might make the mud hold together (adding dry dirt, sand, or grass). Children can use branches and other items for arms and facial features. Keep watch to see what happens to the mud person when it dries in the sun.

Indoor Mud Fun

What's in the mud? Place mud on several pie plates and have children examine it with a magnifying glass. "What is mud made of? Can you see bugs or worms in it?" Remove pebbles and sticks before trying the next activity.

Paint with mud. For a "natural" finger paint, add a little white glue to the mud. Talk about how the mud feels as children paint with it. How does it feel when it's dry?

Remember

• Inform families that you're planning a mud exploration when the weather is right. Ask them to send in a change of old clothes to have on hand.

• Remind threes that this special school activity is not something to do at home without an adult's permission.

• Let children explore with mud in their own ways. Don't insist every child take part in every activity.

BOOKS

Try these books to continue your fun with mud.

• *Mary Ann's Mud Day* by Janice Udry (Harper & Row)

• *The Quicksand Book* by Tomie dePaola (Holiday House)

• *Pete's Puddle* by Joanna Foster (Alfred A. Knopf)

SCIENCE

Put your threes on the trail of something everyone and everything has — a shadow.

SHADOW HUNTING

Aim: Children will use observation and language skills as they investigate the properties of shadows.
Group size: Whole group.
Materials: A battery-powered tape player and music tapes for outdoor use; and mural paper and markers.

GETTING READY

Head outdoors on a sunny day. Children are sure to notice their shadows. When they do, ask, "Who has a shadow? What does it look like? When do you see your shadow? What else has a shad-

ow?" Provide plenty of time for children to respond to each question.

BEGIN

Take a "shadow" walk around the school neighborhood. Look for as many shadows as possible — birds, trees, houses, clothes on a line, cars, signs, people, animals, etc. Does each shadow look just like the person or object? Talk about how the shadows are like the objects and how they are different. Look for shadows of moving cars, people, and animals. Do the shadows change as these things move?

As you walk, look for places where there are no shadows. Have children stand in the shade. Can they see their shadows now? Share ideas on why they can't see their shadows anymore.

If possible, take a morning and an afternoon walk to observe the shadows of the same object, such as that of a playground tree. Does the shadow of the tree look different at different times of the day? Encourage children to suggest ideas of why this change occurs.

Shadow Dancing and Sculptures

Time for a different kind of movement activity. Bring out the tape player. Play music for children to dance to in the sun. As children move, challenge them to find ways to make their shadows taller or shorter. Shout, "Freeze!" As children stand still, have them check to see if their shadow looks like anyone else's.

Tracing Shadows

Find an interesting shadow outside, and demonstrate how to lay mural paper on the shadow and trace it. Then give children paper and markers to do the same. Display the tracings in the room. Together, try to identify the different objects by their shadows.

Remember

▪ It's difficult for threes to recall the size of an object's morning shadow when looking at the afternoon shadow. Trace the morning and afternoon shadows to help children make comparisons.
▪ Investigate shadows on a cloudy day. Can children see their shadows? How do their shadows look different today? Share ideas on why the shadows have changed.

BOOKS

Share these books about shadows with threes.

▪ *Science Fun with a Flashlight* by Herman and Nina Schneider (McGraw-Hill)

▪ *Shadows* by Taro Gami (Heian International)

▪ *What Makes a Shadow?* by Clyde Bulla (Harper & Row)

SCIENCE

Explore the wonderful world of reflection!

MIRROR, MIRROR, ON THE WALL ...

Aim: Children will use observation and experimentation to discover properties of mirrors.

Group size: Three or four children.

Materials: A variety of unbreakable mirrors, such as hand-held, stand-up, and pocket mirrors; other items in which children can see their reflection, such as appliances, windows, metal spoons, foil, and water; and chart paper and a marker.

GETTING READY

Talk about what a *reflection* is. Emphasize the word's meaning by holding up a mirror and saying, "I can see my reflection in this mirror. It's just like a picture of my face!" Then offer the mirror to each child to see his or her reflection, too. Invite a few children at a time to walk around the room with you looking for objects in which they can see their reflections, such as metal appliances, windows, metal spoons, foil, and water.

BEGIN

After your "reflection walk," sit with the children and show them different types of mirrors. Allow plenty of time for children to look into and investigate the mirrors on their own. If children don't discover on their own that they can see themselves, suggest they breathe onto the mirror. What happens? What happens a few seconds after they see their breath on the mirror?

Invite threes to hold the mirrors in different ways, such as in front of their mouths with their mouths open, at arm's length slightly higher than their shoulders, and against a corner of the room. What can they see? Suggest they try holding a mirror outside a doorway while standing inside. What can they see now? Record their discoveries on chart paper. Later, hang the chart in your science center with the mirrors for more independent investigation.

Make a Kaleidoscope

Help children tape three square mirrors together, reflective side in, to form a triangle. Put the mirrors on a piece of white paper and drop some colorful items to form repeated images in the kaleidoscope. Try flower petals, colorful plastic blocks, beads, and other small toys.

Remember

▪ Make sure you use *only* unbreakable mirrors.

▪ Invite older children to look in a mirror while drawing pictures of themselves.

BOOKS

Here are books your threes can "reflect" upon!

▪ *Look Again!* by Tana Hoban (Greenwillow Books)

▪ *Look! Look!* by Tana Hoban (Greenwillow Books)

▪ *My Mirror* by Kay Davies and Wendy Oldfield (Doubleday)

SCIENCE

Threes will enjoy making ants the guests of honor at a feast of discovery!

A PICNIC FOR ANTS

Aim: Children will use observation, prediction, and language skills as they observe ants' eating habits.

Group size: Three or four children at a time to prepare the foods; whole group for observation.

Materials: Large paper plate; plastic sandwich bags; small amounts of several foods to test, such as bread crumbs, cheese, cookie crumbs, fruit, lettuce, sunflower seeds, peanut butter, sugar, and flour; and chart paper and a marker.

GETTING READY

Gather children to talk about ants. Encourage them to share experiences they have had with ants. Ask, "What happens if you leave a piece of food on the ground? Have you ever been on a picnic and had ants come, too? What happened?" Sharing an "ant experience" of your own often helps to get children talking.

Invite children to plan a picnic for the ants. Ask them to name foods they think ants would like. Show the foods you've gathered and have children predict which ones the ants will like best. Record their ideas on chart paper. Then ask, "What size pieces of food do you think the ants want? Why?" Ask children to help tear the solid foods into tiny pieces. Leave a few larger pieces to see what the ants do with them. Place the foods in separate bags for carrying outside.

BEGIN

It's picnic time! Take a walk outside to a place far away from the building. (You don't want to encourage ants near your school!) If possible, locate an active ant hill. Help children arrange the foods on the paper plate.

The ants will need time to discover the food and quiet to know it's safe to come out, so encourage children to move away from the area. Check again every 20-30 minutes to see if the "picnic" is in full swing.

Give children time to study the plate and the ants' behaviors. "Are any of the pieces of food gone? Which foods do they like best? Least?" (You might bring along the chart-paper list for checking children's predictions on the spot.) "What happened to the larger pieces of food? Do the ants ever work together to move these pieces?" Help children focus on the parts of their bodies that ants use to carry the food.

Some children may want to follow the ants to see where they take the food. Others may want to look around the playground for natural items that they think the ants might eat to add to the plate.

Remember

- Threes are good observers but may not have the words to describe what they see. Be a model for them by verbalizing what they see. "Look, the ant is taking the lettuce leaf. I wonder where he will go with it?"
- Sing a few choruses of "The Ants Go Marching One by One" as you watch the picnic parade!

BOOKS

| Share these books to add to the experience. | ■ *Ants Are Fun* by Mildred Myrick (Harper & Row) | ■ *Questions and Answers About Ants* by Millicent Selsam (Scholastic) | ■ *The Way of an Ant* by Kazue Mizumura (Thomas Y. Crowell) |

SCIENCE

There's more than one way to move a heavy load!

HOW CAN WE MOVE THIS BOX OF BLOCKS?

Aim: Children will use observation and problem-solving skills as they experiment with simple machines.
Group size: Three or four children.
Materials: A cardboard or lightweight wooden box to fill with blocks, a small wagon or dolly, a small sled, a rope, and a large stick to use as a lever.

GETTING READY

Gather a small group of children and ask for their help with a job. Tell them that you want to move a box of blocks from the block area to the opposite end of the room. Ask them to first fill the box with blocks.

BEGIN

Now have the children try moving the box of blocks. They'll likely be surprised at how heavy it has become. Ask, "How can we move this heavy box?" Be patient as children think of ideas. Try their ideas, such as pushing it. Talk about whether pushing the box seems to be the best way to move it.

Show children a rope and ask how they might use it to move the box. Again, give children time to come up with ideas. Try their ideas, such as attaching the rope to the box and pulling it together. Ask, "Is this way any easier?" Encourage children to think of ways to move the box so they won't have to work so hard.

Bring out a small, flat plastic sled or a large plastic tray. Let children examine the item, then invite them to suggest a way to use it to move the box. Try their ideas, such as putting the box on it. Decide together if moving the box is getting easier. Can they think of something that would make the job even easier?

Bring out the wagon or dolly. Talk about why the wheels will make the box easier to move. Then present children with another problem: How will they get the heavy box on the wagon? Let them try different ways to pick up the box, being careful that they don't hurt themselves.

Then show children the stick and a block. Explain that the stick is a simple tool called a lever, and that the lever and block can help them pick up the box. Encourage children to experiment with the lever to see if they can figure out how to use it. Then, if necessary, show them how to slide it under one end of the box while putting a block under the stick. When they press down on the stick the box will rise up.

Time to put the heavy box on the wagon! Talk about their success. Give children plenty of time to "ride" the box around in the wagon. They've worked hard to get to this end!

Remember

▪ Keep a watchful eye throughout this activity so that little fingers don't get caught under the box. The box should be heavy enough that children cannot move it easily but not so heavy that they could strain and hurt themselves.
▪ Extend the experience by providing small wheel toys in the block area for children to experiment with transporting different-sized loads of blocks.

BOOKS

Use these titles to continue your discussion of wheels.

▪ *Big Wheels* by Anne Rockwell (Macmillan)

▪ *Cars and Trucks and Things That Go* by Richard Scarry (Western)

▪ *The Pop-Up Book of Trucks* by Loretta Lustig (Random House)

SCIENCE

Fours will think this activity is just for fun, but you'll know they're using a key science skill.

JOIN IN AN OBSERVATION GAME!

Aim: Children will use observation, creative-thinking, and language skills as they observe an unusual sight.

Group size: Whole group.

Materials: An assortment of odd clothing items and other objects to make into a strange costume (for example, two hats, shorts to wear over pants, mismatched shoes or boots, and an upside-down broomstick), chart paper, and a marker.

In Advance: Arrange for an adult (an aide or a family member) to visit the room for a minute or two wearing a very strange costume. Be sure to explain the purpose of the activity and point out that he or she can also make noises and/or unusual movements and motions.

GETTING READY

At circle time, tell children they'll have a special visitor today. Explain that this person will look unusual and that this is all part of a special game. The rules are to look very carefully at the visitor and see how many strange things they notice about the person. Present the visitor in an amusing way so children are not frightened by her appearance.

BEGIN

Welcome the visitor and watch the children's reactions. Let them observe for a minute or two and then say goodbye.

Encourage children to take time to think about what they saw, then invite them to share what they recall about the visitor. Record their observations on chart paper. Ask, "What made that person unusual? What did she do?" Draw on children's descriptive language by asking them to think about specifics, such as the colors, shapes, and sizes of clothing the visitor wore or objects she carried. Add these to your chart.

Now bring the visitor back into the room so that children can check their observations. What things did they remember most clearly? What did they forget?

More Observation Fun

Use this same technique to observe other things in the room. For example, encourage children to look at a new pet, helping them focus with questions: "How does our hamster move in the cage? How does it hold food to eat? When does it sleep? What does it look like when it's sleeping?" Record the children's observations. Some children may want to draw pictures of what they see.

Ask volunteers to take turns being observed by the group, who name descriptive features. (Stress *friendly* observations.) For example: "Sean has red hair. He's wearing jeans and a green shirt. He smiles a lot."

Remember

▪ Observing for detail is a skill children need for present and future reading, math, and science learning. Language skills also get a workout as they communicate what they've seen.

▪ Fours tend to remember best what they observed most recently. To encourage closer observation, show an unusual object at circle time, then ask children to recall what they remember about the object at the end of the day. Repeat this procedure frequently.

BOOKS

Books are another way to build observation skills. Try these.

▪ *Each Peach Pear Plum* by Janet Ahlberg (Viking Penguin)

▪ *Take Another Look* by Tana Hoban (Greenwillow Books)

▪ *What Is Your Favorite Thing To See?* by Myra Gibson (Grosset & Dunlap)

SCIENCE

Build on fours' natural interest in filling containers for an exciting science experiment.

PREDICTING WITH CONTAINERS AND SAND

Aim: Children will use observation, comparison, measurement, and prediction skills as they experiment with sand and containers.

Group size: Four or five children.

Materials: Sand table or dishpan of sand, a variety of different-shaped plastic bowls, bottles, cardboard boxes, chart paper, and a marker.

GETTING READY

Talk about predictions. Ask, "What is a *prediction*? How do you make a prediction?" Give children time to share their ideas, then explain as needed that a prediction is a kind of smart guess. For example, a weatherperson predicts rain based on having observed conditions that made it rain in the past. Talk about how we make predictions in the same way — by watching something and then making a guess based on what we've seen before. Brainstorm some ways children predict every day, such as how many blocks to use in a tower so it won't fall down, how hard to roll a ball to knock something down, how a story will end, etc.

BEGIN

Introduce the containers and let children play freely with them in the sand. This exercise will give children experience with the amount each container holds. Then gather children and point to each container. Which ones did children find hold a lot of sand and which hold only a little?

Make a chart with a simple outline of each container. Invite children to predict which container will hold the *most* sand. Have each child make a mark on the chart next to the container he or she chooses.

Next, ask children to take turns filling the containers with sand using a measuring cup. Count together as each container is filled and record the number of cups it holds on the chart. Compare the results with the predictions. Star the container that holds the most sand. Then invite children to repeat the experiment, this time predicting and testing to see which container holds the least amount of sand.

Does the Shape Matter?

Collect boxes of similar size but different shape. Ask children to predict whether the boxes will hold more, less, or the same amount of sand. Have children experiment to test their predictions.

Remember

• Predicting is an important thinking skill. To make a prediction children must use information they have gained before and apply it to a new situation. This involves flexible thinking as children draw on old information and use it in a new way.

• Don't expect predictions to be accurate. The aim of this activity is to help children learn through experience to observe and make thoughtful guesses.

• Look for opportunities to have children make predictions in everyday activities. Always record their ideas and return to check the predictions.

BOOKS

Look for these books with additional science suggestions for teachers.	• *Mudpies to Magnets* by Williams, Rockwell, and Sherwood (Gryphon House)	• *Watching and Wondering* (Minnesota Mathematics and Science Teaching Project)	• *What Will Happen If...* by Sprung, Froschl, and Campbell (Educational Equity Concepts)

SCIENCE

Fours will feel like real scientists as they try these evaporation experiments.

WHERE DOES THE WATER GO?

Aim: Children will use observation, prediction, measurement, and language skills as they experiment with water and evaporation.
Group size: Four or five children.
Materials: Chalk, dark construction or blotter paper, water, two glasses, yarn, chart paper, and a marker.

GETTING READY

Choose a time after a recent rain to introduce this activity. Talk about the rain. Ask, "Will the things that got wet in the rain stay wet? What happens to the water?" Introduce the word *evaporation* and define it as the process that dries things when they are wet.

BEGIN

Ask, "What do you think happens to puddles after it stops raining? How fast do you think they dry up?" Go outside in the morning and choose a puddle to observe. Give children chalk for tracing a circle around the outside edge of the puddle. Ask if they think the puddle will change in size by lunchtime. Record the children's predictions in a notebook and transfer to chart paper back in the room. Later, go back outside to check whether the puddle has changed.

If the puddle is not all dried up, trace the outline again and make another prediction. Come back frequently to check the puddle and to continue tracing. If the puddle is large enough, continue the process through the next day. When the puddle is dry, review together the series of smaller and smaller chalk circles. Remind children that each circle shows how the water in the puddle got

reduced to less and less. Ask, "Where do you think the water went? What do you think helped dry up the puddle?" Give children plenty of time to offer their ideas.

Indoor Experiments

You can also try a variation of the puddle activity inside. Pour a small amount of water onto a large sheet of dark-colored construction or blotter paper. Make repeated tracings of the outside of the wet area with chalk, as you did with the puddle.

Here's another evaporation experiment to do inside. Have children fill two clear glasses with equal amounts of water, then measure the height of the water in each glass with yarn or string. Place these pieces vertically on separate sheets of paper. Then put one glass in a sunny window and another in a closet. Have interested children check the glasses, making a new measurement each time with fresh yarn. Place these pieces in order next to the first ones to help children see that the water is disappearing. Discuss in which glass it evaporates more quickly. Ask children to give their ideas on what makes the difference.

Remember

■ Most fours think evaporation is "magic." This activity can help them begin to understand what really causes it. It's not important for them to grasp all the related scientific principles. Concentrate on helping them see that things like sunlight and time make wet things become dry.

BOOKS

Try these books for more experiments to do with fours.

■ *An Activities Handbook for Teaching Young Children* by Doreen Croft and R. Hess (Houghton Mifflin)

■ *Mudpies to Magnets* by Williams, Rockwell, and Sherwood (Gryphon House)

■ *Rainy Day* by Imogene Forte (Kid's Stuff)

SCIENCE

Use children's natural fascination with magnets to do some exciting experiments!

FUN WITH MAGNETS

Aim: Children will use observation, prediction, and experimentation skills as they work with magnets.

Group size: Four to six children.

Materials: A variety of magnets in different sizes and shapes; cardboard or plastic-foam trays, paper, markers, and masking tape; and magnetic and non-magnetic items (paper clips, screws, buttons, feathers, sponges, washers, pennies, brass fasteners, etc.).

GETTING READY

Encourage experimentation with magnets by inviting children to go on a Magnetic Scavenger Hunt. Give each a magnet and some masking tape. Ask children to test items in the room to find ones the magnet will stick to, and encourage them to put tape on those objects.

Gather the group to discuss the children's findings. "What did the magnet stick to? What didn't it stick to?" Find the items children identified and list each on chart paper. Review the list together. Do children see any similarities among the items? Are they the same size? Are they made of the same kind of material?

BEGIN

Place magnetic and non-magnetic items on a tray in the center of a table. Display different magnets and let children examine their differences. Do they think some will be stronger than others? Which ones? Why?

Label one tray "Yes" for items children think will be attracted to the magnets and another "No" for non-magnetic items. Encourage predictions based on earlier discussions and experiences.

Give children time to test their predictions. Were they right? Which items stuck to the magnets? Which items fooled them? Invite children to explain why some objects stick to magnets while others don't.

Invite children to look for other items in the room that they did not test during the hunt earlier. Challenge them to choose an item that they think will be magnetic and one that won't. Can they stump others?

Make Your Own Magnets

Use a paper clip and a strong magnet to create your own magnet. First straighten the paper clip. Rub the magnet over the paper clip — always moving in the same direction — at least 25 times. Now invite children to test their homemade magnets. How do they work?

Remember

▪ Magnets are a confusing yet exciting phenomenon for fours. Remember that the focus of this activity is to work with magnets and observe their effects. If some children begin to grasp that material makes the difference in whether an object does or doesn't stick to a magnet, encourage that line of thinking. But remember that what's most important is to involve children in the process of experimenting and testing their ideas, not to get the correct answers.

▪ Encourage children to look for magnets at home. They may find the magnets in cabinet or refrigerator doors, plus the ones holding up their paintings on the refrigerator!

BOOKS

Add these books to your science collection.	▪ *Magnets* by Illa Podendorf (Children's Press)	▪ *Magnets and How to Use Them* by Tillie S. Pine (Scholastic)	▪ *The Real Book of Magnets* by Mae Freeman (Scholastic)

SCIENCE

Young scientists investigate melting — without snow!

TAKING THE HEAT

Aim: Children will use observation, prediction, evaluation, and language skills to investigate the fastest way to melt an ice cube.
Group size: Three or four children.
Materials: Ice cubes, plastic containers, paper cups and plates, aluminum foil, cloth scraps, plastic wrap, water, sand, chart paper and a marker, and small pieces of chocolate (optional).

GETTING READY

Gather children for a discussion on things that melt. Ask, "What happens when you put ice in a glass of water? What happens when you bring a snowball inside? What happens if you leave crayons out in the sun?" If you're feeling brave, give each child a small piece of chocolate to hold in one hand during this discussion. Ask, "What do you think makes ice melt? What makes crayons melt?" Give children plenty of time to share their ideas, then invite everyone to look at their hands. Ask, "What happened to the chocolate? What do you think made it melt?"

BEGIN

Show children a tray of ice and ask them to think of different ways to melt each cube. Record their ideas on chart paper, then ask children to predict which method will work the fastest and which the slowest. Try the methods for which you have materials. For example, place an ice cube in a container of cold water, one in hot water, and one in sand or snow. Next, you might wrap the ice cubes in different materials, such as aluminum foil, plastic wrap, and cloth, then predict which cubes will melt the fastest.

For each experiment, always record predictions, experiment, and then refer back to the children's predictions. Talk about which methods work the best and star these on the chart.

Try It Again

Another day, experiment by placing ice cubes in different spots around the room. Ask children to help you decide where to test the cubes, such as on a sunny window, in a dark closet, inside a refrigerator, outside a window, and near a heater or air conditioner. Ask them to rank the places by how fast they think the ice will melt in that spot to how slow they think the ice will melt there, and record the predictions on chart paper. When the cubes have all melted, check the chart. Discuss why a particular cube melted faster than

another. What conclusions can children draw about what makes things melt? Encourage everyone to share their ideas.

Remember

■ Keep the focus of these activities on the conditions that are needed for objects to melt — mainly a heat source. Don't try to bring in factors about the amount of heat needed to melt different materials. It's more advanced than you need to be right now.
■ On a snowy day, empty the water table and fill it with snow. Children can play with it and watch it melt. How much water will a box full of snow make? Have children test and find out.

BOOKS

Share these books to enhance the experience.

■ *All Wet! All Wet!* by James Skofield (Harper & Row)

■ *Ice Is ... Whee!* by Carol Greene (Children's Press)

■ *Water Is Wet!* by Sally Cartwright (Coward, McCann & Geoghegan)

SCIENCE

Send fours outdoors with paper streamers to find evidence of the wind.

BE WIND DETECTIVES!

Aim: Children will use observation, creative-thinking, and language skills as they investigate the wind.

Group size: Whole group.

Materials: Tape and two-inch-wide strips of newsprint or colored party steamers about two to three feet long. There should be one strip for each child.

In Advance: Prepare the streamers or strips of paper.

GETTING READY

Plan this activity for a moderately windy day. Make the wind the topic at circle time. Ask, "Can you see the wind? How do you know when the wind is blowing?" Give children plenty of time to offer their ideas. Then read a book about the wind, such as *Gilberto and the Wind* by Marie Hall Ets, *The Hat* by Tomi Ungerer, or one of those listed below. Invite children to name objects they have seen the wind blow.

BEGIN

Give each child a streamer, then head outdoors. Give children time to experiment with the streamers to see what they can do with them. Ask, "Can you use the streamers to tell if the wind is blowing? Try and see." Watch to see what ideas children come up with. Invite volunteers to share their methods with the others. Ask, "Can you tell from your streamer how hard the wind is blowing? How can you tell?"

If children haven't already tried this, encourage them to run with the streamers. What happens when they run fast? When they run slowly?

Tape some streamers to the climbers or to the branches of a tree and observe them. What happens when the wind stops?

Sing a Breezy Song

Here's a song to sing about your wind adventures. It's to the tune of "Twinkle Twinkle Little Star."

> *Today the wind came out to play.*
> *We played together all the day.*
> *It blew my streamers in the air,*
> *I felt it blowing through my hair.*
> *It blew a cloud behind a tree,*
> *But most of all it played with me!*

Remember

▪ Observing the wind can also be a quiet activity. On a warm and windy day, find a comfortable place on the playground to sit and watch the wind. Ask children to listen for the sounds the wind makes and to observe how it moves the trees, grass, bushes, etc. After a few minutes, ask, "What did you see or hear that told you there was wind on the playground?" Fours will be using those important observation skills again.

▪ You can use paper and cloth of different weights to test how strong the wind is blowing. Let children experiment with these items to see which take just a little breeze to move them and which need a strong wind.

BOOKS

Share these other books with wind and air themes.	▪ *Curious George Flies a Kite* by Margaret Rey (Houghton Mifflin)	▪ *When the Wind Stops* by Charlotte Zolotow (Harper & Row)	▪ *The Wind Blew* by Pat Hutchins (Macmillan)

SCIENCE

Fours create their own "piece of the earth" with this science activity.

PLANTING TERRARIUMS

Aim: Children will use observation, experimentation, and prediction skills as they create a natural setting.

Group size: Three or four children.

Materials: Large, clear plastic cups and/or plastic shoeboxes or glass aquariums; potting soil, gravel or small stones, shells, and bark; plastic wrap; spray water bottles; small houseplants or cuttings, moss, and ferns; and small toy animals and people (optional).

In Advance: Collect cuttings from your own plants at home. Invite families to send in cuttings, too. A local florist might also donate small cuttings.

GETTING READY

Gather a small group together and show them the plant cuttings. Explain that you'll use them in a *terrarium*. Show children a completed terrarium and point out that it's like a little piece of nature. Talk about what you find when you dig in the ground or walk in a garden. Show children how a terrarium is made up of the same things — dirt, rocks, plants, water, and air.

BEGIN

Give each child a plastic cup. Have each place a small amount of gravel in the bottom, then add soil and stones. Be sure children don't add too much. When the plants are added, they should be well below the top of the cup to create a protected environment.

Next, take a cutting and help children identify the roots. Have each child place one or two cuttings in the soil, checking to be sure that all the roots are covered. Add some moss around the plants to help hold water, then have children spray the plants lightly with water. Place the terrariums in a sunny window.

As children observe their plants over time, discuss what they think makes the plants grow. Ask children to predict what would happen if they kept a terrarium in the sunlight but didn't water it, or if they gave a plant water but kept it in a dark closet. Test both scenarios with extra terrariums that you have made. What can children conclude about what plants need?

Make a Class Terrarium

Use a plastic shoebox or a glass aquarium to make a bigger terrarium. In this larger space, children can create hills and valleys and add props to create a scene. Keep in the moisture by covering the top with plastic wrap, and spray only when the dirt appears dry.

Remember

▪ Keep the terrariums in school for a while so children can practice taking care of them. The biggest danger to a terrarium is too much water. Explain to children that they don't need as much water as houseplants because these plants are protected inside the container.

▪ This can be a time to talk about pollution and why it's important to recycle and do other things to protect nature. Point out that your terrariums are free of garbage and pollution. Encourage children to think of things people can do to make the earth cleaner and healthier.

BOOKS

Share these books about plants and protecting the earth.

▪ *The Little Park* by Dale Fife (Albert Whitman)

▪ *The Tree* by Donald Carrick (Macmillan)

▪ *Wilson's World* by Edith T. Hurd (Harper & Row)

SCIENCE

Fours can harvest a lot of learning from watching worms.

BUILD A WORM FARM

Aim: Children will use observation and prediction skills as they study a member of the animal world.

Group size: Four or five children; whole group to collect worms.

Materials: A large glass jar and a smaller one that fits inside it; soil; sand; large spoons; a paper bag; and coffee grounds, leaves, and lettuce (worm food).

GETTING READY

Gather children to talk about worms. Ask, "Where do worms live? In what kind of weather do you see worms?" Invite children to share where they've seen worms.

Invite volunteers to imitate how worms move. Have them imagine they're worms moving through the earth. Create a pile of pillows for them to "worm" through. Point out that worms are important because as they wiggle through the soil, they turn it over. Explain that churning up the soil makes it healthier.

BEGIN

Invite children to help build a home for worms and observe them for a while. Ask a few interested children to help fill a large glass jar with alternate layers of sand and soil. (Children will more easily see how worms mix up dirt as they move through it.) When the jar is half full, place the smaller jar inside it. (It will stop the worms from burrowing into places where they can't be observed.) Continue filling the large jar to within a few inches of the top.

The best time to find worms is after a spring rain. If you dig for worms, look for areas where the earth is loose. Transport them with a little soil.

Put the worms in the large jar, along with small amounts of some food(s) listed above. As children observe the worms, ask, "What do you think it's like underground where worms live? Do you think the home we've made for the worms is like what they're used to?" Give children time to share their ideas. If no one mentions darkness, ask, "Do you think it's dark underground? How could we make it darker for our worms?" Try as many of the children's ideas as possible to find one that works best. A paper bag over the jar is an easy way to simulate darkness.

Check the food supply daily. Remove rotting pieces. Every few days, sprinkle water on the soil so it's moist but *not* wet. Worms can drown in too much water.

Watch for signs of burrows made by the worms and for mixing of the sand and soil. Record children's daily observations. Review these together now and then for reminders of behaviors fours have found interesting.

Remember

▪ Help children to recognize that worms are an essential part of the earth's ecosystem. Demonstrate your respect for worms by treating them with care. And after a few weeks, return them to the same general area where you found them. It sends the wrong message to children about the value of all life when we take creatures from the earth, then let them die.

▪ Some children may be afraid to touch worms. Don't force them. But be sure children who do wash their hands afterwards.

BOOKS

| Here are more science books with interesting ideas. | ▪ *Hug a Tree* by Rockwell, Sherwood, and Williams (Gryphon House) | ▪ *Weather and Seasons* by Lynn Cohen (Monday Morning Books) | ▪ *What Will Happen If ... ?* by Sprung, Froschl, and Campbell (Educational Equity Concepts) |

SCIENCE

Help fours to understand that every plant has its place in our world.

ADOPT A WEED

Aim: Children will observe, compare, measure, and predict the growth of a "pet" plant.
Group size: Four to six children.
Materials: Yarn or string, chart and drawing paper, crayons, scissors, tape, seeds (such as squash, peas, or green beans), rinsed yogurt cups, and potting soil.

GETTING READY

This is a good activity to introduce early in the spring. Talk about the new season by asking, "Have you noticed any changes outside? Are there any new plants growing on the playground?" If possible, bring in plants or pictures of plants children might see outdoors. Then invite children to "adopt" a weed on the playground and watch as it grows.

BEGIN

Take a Weed Walk

During playground times, take small groups of children on an "Adopt-a-Weed" walk. Choose a weed that is in a semi-protected area. (You might choose one weed for the whole group or let the small groups each select their own.) Let children observe and carefully examine the weed by smelling and touching it. (Be sure children don't taste plant parts. Many are toxic to humans.) Bring along paper and crayons (and a hard surface to draw on) so children can draw pictures of the weed if they wish. Record their descriptions and comments about the weed in a notebook. Transfer these later to chart paper. Use yarn or string to measure the height of the weed, then tape it to chart paper back in the room. Date the strip, as well as the drawings and observations.

Check the weed's progress every few days. Repeat the process of observing and drawing. Graph its growth by using yarn or string to measure the height each time. Paste the strings next to the original measurement on chart paper in order to show the progressive growth of the plant. This helps children see the pattern of growth.

Weeding Indoors

Display the various drawings and charts in your science area, along with picture reference books on plants and weeds. Ask children to predict how tall the weed will be when it stops growing. Give them yarn or string cut to the length of their predictions. Label each with the child's name and hang it in the science area. Invite fours to compare their prediction with the weed's current measurement.

Which Are Taller — Plants or Weeds?

Give children potting soil, plant seeds, and empty yogurt containers. Assist each in starting a plant to compare with the adopted weed. Along with observations of the stages in a plant's growth, children can predict which will grow taller, their plant or the adopted weed.

Remember

▪ Children may have heard family members complaining about weeds. Talk about why weeds are pulled from a garden (so they don't take away nutrients from flower or vegetable plants). Help children understand that weeds have value as plants and aren't always "bad."

BOOKS

Share more books about plants with fours.	▪ *Alligator's Garden* by Muntean and Rubel (Dial Books)	▪ *The Carrot Seed* by Ruth Krauss (Harper & Row)	▪ *What Should I Put in the Hole I Dig?* by Eleanor Thompson (Albert Whitman)

SCIENCE

Children are fascinated to find out there's a real skeleton inside their bodies!

WHAT'S INSIDE OF ME?

Aim: Children will use observation skills to learn about the skeletons inside their bodies.

Group size: A small group.

Materials: A flashlight; books with large, clear pictures of skeletons; and a plastic model of a human skeleton (optional).

In Advance: Contact a high school or college biology department about borrowing a model of a human skeleton. Models can also be purchased (though not inexpensively) through science supply companies.

GETTING READY

Share a book, such as *Look Inside Your Body* by Gina Ingoglia or other age-appropriate books about skeletons, with children. Encourage them to look at the pictures and to ask questions about what they see. Place the book where children can look at it whenever they'd like.

BEGIN

When children express interest in skeletons and bones, discuss them. Invite children to try to feel their bones under their skin. Search first for bones in easy-to-find places such as fingers, elbows, noses, chins, knees, and ankles. Then ask, "Why do you think we have bones? What do you think would happen if we didn't have bones? What do you think bones look like?" Pause after each question and allow plenty of time for children to share their ideas and/or concerns.

Follow up with this poem. Invite children to act out some of the words.

> *There are bones in my fingers,*
> *There are bones in my toes.*
> *When I feel my face,*
> *I feel bones in my nose.*
>
> *Fish have bones,*
> *So do pelicans.*
> *And when we put our bones together,*
> *They make skeletons!*

Extension: Examine a Real Skeleton

Place a model of a human skeleton in your science area. Observe children as they approach it, and note the kinds of things they're curious about and whether some children seem frightened by it. Talk about the skeleton and the different bones that make up the human body.

Bring in a flashlight and invite children to hold it very close to their hands with the light on. Often they'll be able to see the bones in their hands right through their skin!

Remember

- Some Halloween images make skeletons seem very frightening. Help children deal with confused feelings about skeletons by showing them what they really are.

BOOKS

Here are three good children's books about body parts.

- *First Facts About Your Body* by Caroline Arnold (Ladybird Books)
- *Look Inside Your Body* by Gina Ingoglia (Grosset & Dunlap)
- *Where Is Your Nose?* by Laura Rader (Putnam & Grosset)

SCIENCE

Turn a drizzly day into a science adventure.

LET IT RAIN!

Aim: Children will use observation, exploration, and language skills as they experiment with water.
Group size: Four or five children.
Materials: Several spray bottles filled with water; a dishpan or water table; soft, fat, absorbent sponges; an empty coffee can; popsicle sticks; and paper and crayons.

GETTING READY

Talk about the weather at circle time. Ask, "Did anybody get wet coming to school today?" Invite children to share their rainy-day stories.

Listen for the kinds of questions children ask about rain. When they seem curious about what makes rain, try this activity to build understanding.

BEGIN

Explain to children that even when it's not raining, there's water in the air. We can't see it, but it's called water vapor. Clouds contain water vapor, too. When the clouds get so full of water vapor that they can't hold it all, it falls to the ground as rain.

Gather children around the water table or a dishpan. Give each a sponge and explain that the sponges are clouds. Spray the sponges very lightly with water so they're barely damp. Explain that these are clouds on a dry day. Have children squeeze the sponges to see if anything comes out.

Invite children to continue spraying the sponges so that their "clouds" fill up with "water vapor." Let them spray until they think their cloud is so full it will start raining. Ask children how they can tell their sponges are full of water. When they're ready, have them squeeze to produce a "rainstorm." Compare the sponges now to how they felt full of water.

Give children plenty of time to experiment with the sponge clouds. Use colored water with white sponges to show even more vividly how the clouds absorb water.

Make a Rain Gauge

Place a coffee can in an open area of the playground on a rainy day. When the rain stops, or on the next day, measure the amount of rain collected. Have two volunteers stand a popsicle stick in the water, then mark the wet line with a crayon. Paste the stick on paper and note the date. Repeat the process on other rainy days. Place the new stick to the right each time to create a bar graph. Talk about the results.

Remember

▪ Fives don't need to know the whole water cycle to understand how clouds and rain are related. Some children may make the connection between evaporation experiments and this cloud activity. Help them to see that as the water evaporates from the ground, it collects in clouds.
▪ Tracking rainfall over several days or weeks is the kind of long-range project that fives enjoy. It lets them refer back to and compare their own findings.
▪ Examine the collected rainwater with a microscope or powerful magnifying glass. What do children see in the water? Compare it to magnified tap water.

BOOKS

| Add these books to your discussions about rain. | ▪ *And It Rained* by Ellen Raski (Atheneum) | ▪ *Rain* by Peter Spier (Doubleday) | ▪ *Rainy Day Together* by Ellen Parson (Harper & Row) |

SCIENCE

Help fives understand the abstract concept of temperature.

EXPERIMENTING WITH TEMPERATURE

Aim: Children will observe and predict temperature changes and their effects.
Group size: Four or five children.
Materials: Water, three large bowls, ice cubes, metal spoons, paper cups, thermometers, chart paper, and markers.

GETTING READY

On a day when it is very hot or very cold out and children are talking about feeling hot or cold, ask, "How do we know when the weather is cold or hot? What do you use at home to know what the temperature is?"

When children express an interest in finding out more about temperature, try these activities.

BEGIN

Fill one paper cup with hot water and the other cup with cold. Invite children to feel the outside of the cups and to choose the one that they think is warmer. Mark a red dot on that cup.

Now use metal spoons as thermometers. Pass the three spoons around so each child can feel if they're hot, warm, or cool. Then, ask a child to place one spoon in each cup and leave one out of the water. Ask children to predict what will happen to each spoon and record their ideas. Leave the spoons in the water for one minute, then remove. Ask children to test how the wet spoons feel compared with the dry spoon. Check the predictions together to see if anyone guessed what would happen.

A Temperature Trick

Here's another experiment to try. Fill three bowls with cold, room-temperature, and warm water, respectively. Place them on a table in that order.

Have one child put a hand in the cold water and describe how it feels. Then, leaving that hand in the cold water, have the child place his other hand in the warm water and describe how it feels. Finally, have the child put *both* hands in the room-temperature water. Ask, "How do your hands feel now?" (The cold hand will feel warm and the warm hand will feel cold.) Let each child have a turn with the experiment.

Using Thermometers

Fill each of four paper cups with water that is very warm, warm, cold, and very cold (add ice cubes). Ask children to feel the outside of each cup and to arrange the cups from hottest to coldest. Next, put a thermometer in each cup and wait a few minutes. Remove and compare the different levels of mercury. Ask, "What would you use a thermometer for?" Encourage children to share times when they've seen family members use thermometers.

Remember

- Show children how to use thermometers carefully. They're breakable and the mercury inside is poisonous.
- Keep the water in the bowls at very different temperatures so children can make comparisons easily.
- Expand the concept of temperature by using many bowls of water to seriate from coolest to warmest.

BOOKS

Add these books to your science center.

- *Science Fun* by Imogene Forte (Incentive Publications)

- *Who Likes It Hot?* by Mary Garlick (Scholastic)

- *Why You Feel Hot, Why You Feel Cold: Your Body's Temperature* by James Barry (Little, Brown)

SCIENCE

Planting bulbs in the fall makes for an exciting spring!

PLANTING BULBS

Aim: Children will use observation, classification, measurement, and language skills as they engage in a long-term nature project.

Group size: Four to six children.

Materials: Outdoor bulbs such as tulip, daffodil, or crocus; indoor bulbs such as paper-white narcissus or amaryllis (available at garden, discount, or grocery stores); familiar seeds, such as apple, orange, and pumpkin; small shovels, trowels, or big spoons; indoor flower pots or shallow bowls; potting soil or water; marbles or pebbles; chart paper and a marker; and yarn.

GETTING READY

Set out a variety of plant bulbs and seeds in the science area. Let children examine them on their own for a few days. Listen for the kinds of questions and discussions children have about these

items, and especially for interest in planting them. Then gather a small group to talk about the seeds and bulbs. Ask, "How are seeds and bulbs different? How are they alike?" Record children's observations on chart paper.

Explain that one big difference between bulbs and seeds is that bulbs are planted in the fall and seeds are planted in the spring. The bulbs sleep through the winter underground, then bloom in spring. Invite a few children at a time to help you plant some bulbs.

BEGIN

Follow instructions for planting on the bulb packages. Ask children to help you find an area with the kind of soil and light the plants will need. Try to also select a protected area where the bulbs won't be walked on. Plant most bulbs about five inches down and about three to five inches apart. Be sure to let the children do the work!

Remind children that the bulbs will not show any signs of growth for quite a while. Help interested fives use children's science resource books to find out more about bulbs while they wait. When spring weather arrives, visit the bulb garden frequently to watch for signs of growth. Use yarn to measure the bulbs' progress once they sprout.

Plant an Indoor Bulb Garden

If you don't have a protected area outside, create an indoor bulb garden. Narcissus bulbs are the easiest to grow inside. Plant in soil in flowerpots or place in a clear, shallow bowl filled with marbles or pebbles and about two inches of water. Nestle the bulbs upright among the marbles/pebbles and keep water about halfway up the bulb at all times. This method lets children watch how the roots take form while also observing the plant's normal growth.

Remember

- Outdoor bulbs must be planted in the fall to have time to take root. Ask children to help make a map of the area where the bulbs are planted. Record the number in the ground to watch for in the spring.
- Some bulbs are treated with chemicals to preserve and help them grow. Be sure children wash their hands after examining or planting the bulbs. Many bulbs, including all of those suggested in the activity, are poisonous if ingested. Observe to make sure children do not taste or swallow pieces of bulb.

BOOKS

Try other planting ideas in these science activity books for children.

- *From Petals to Pinecones* by Katherine Cutler (Lothrop, Lee & Shepard)

- *Growing Up Green* by Alice Skelsey (Workman Publications)

- *Science Fun* by Imogene Forte (Incentive Publications)

SCIENCE

If your fives love dinosaurs, they'll "dig" this activity!

SANDBOX SCIENTISTS

Aim: Children will use problem-solving, creative-thinking, dramatic-play, and language skills as they take on the roles of special kinds of scientists.

Group size: Four or five children.

Materials: Sandbox; items similar to dinosaur bones to hide in the sand, such as popsicle sticks, plastic-foam pieces, and chicken or turkey bones (boiled to sterilize); paper plates; and chart paper and a marker.

In Advance: Before children arrive, hide the "dinosaur bones" deep in the sandbox. Cover them until activity time. Have extra items on hand to provide more bones as children take their turns with the activity.

GETTING READY

This is an activity to introduce when children have been showing a lot of interest in dinosaurs. It might be one you do after a visit to a dinosaur collection in a museum.

Invite children to tell what they know about the jobs of archaeologists and paleontologists. Record their responses on chart paper. Add to their ideas as needed to help them understand that these scientists look for objects buried in the earth that can tell about life long ago. One thing they look for is the bones of animals, such as dinosaurs. Show pictures of museum dinosaur skeletons or recall with children the dinosaur bones they saw on their visit.

BEGIN

Gather children around the sandbox. Ask how they think scientists would dig for bones and fossils. What tools would they use? Would they work quickly or carefully? Provide time for children to share and discuss their ideas.

Now ask them to imagine that the sandbox is an area where scientists think dinosaur bones may be buried. Invite interested fives to work together to dig for bones. Provide paper plates for collecting the "findings."

When the "bones" have been excavated, talk with children about what they think scientists do with the objects they find. Do they examine them? Listen to their ideas, then encourage children to do the same with their findings. They might sort and classify the items or pretend to be a scientist puzzling over the bones of a strange new creature. Let children follow up the excavation exercise in their own ways.

Remember

▪ Fives tend to be very interested in the jobs of scientists who study objects, fossils, and bones from the past. If possible, visit a natural history museum or check with a museum's education department to see if it has archaeologists or anthropologists who work with young children and will visit your program. Don't worry about children understanding everything they hear or see. Keep the presentation short and hands-on. Then provide lots of opportunities indoors and outdoors for children to go on "digs" of their own.

▪ Art is a good follow-up to the sandbox dig. Ask, "What colors do you think dinosaurs were? Why would they be that color?" Invite children to draw pictures of dinosaurs in the colors or patterns they imagine.

BOOKS

Share these books with children who want to know more about dinosaurs.

▪ *Dinosaurs* by Gail Gibbons (Holiday)

▪ *Dinosaurs* by Gena Neilson (Lauri, Inc.)

▪ *Dinosaurs Are Different* by Aliki (Thomas Y. Crowell)

SCIENCE

A rock is a rock is a rock, right? Not quite!

BE "ROCK HOUNDS"

Aim: Children will use observation, classification, prediction, and problem-solving skills as they identify the characteristics of different rocks.

Group size: Whole group for walk; four to six children for follow-up activities.

Materials: A variety of interesting rocks; magnifying glasses; paper plates, paper bags, chart paper, and a marker; and a pan balance scale (optional).

GETTING READY

This is a great activity to introduce after one child brings in an interesting stone and gets everyone focused on rocks. Invite the group to go on a walk to find their own rocks to study. Give each child a paper bag for holding rocks and set one rule before leaving: You must be able to carry the rocks you find. (This solves the problem of the child who takes too many or wants to collect a boulder-sized rock.) Encourage children to look for rocks of different sizes, shapes, and colors.

BEGIN

Spread out the rocks children have found in the science area. If necessary, have children wash or brush excess dirt off the rocks. Then set out materials for studying the rocks, such as magnifying glasses for close observation and paper plates for sorting them by size, texture, shape, and color. Let children engage in these activities freely. Observe in the center to see what kinds of classification schemes they devise or what discoveries they make about unusual particles, even fossil prints, in the rocks. Record their comments and discoveries on chart paper. Keep a running list of all the different ways the group finds to classify the rocks.

If one is available, place a pan balance scale in the center for comparing the weights of various rocks. Show children as needed how to use the scale. Challenge them to predict which rocks will be the heaviest or lightest, then test their predictions.

Open a Rock Museum

After studying the rocks, children might like to create a rock museum. Work with interested children to select the rocks for the museum. Select those with unique features or ones that are the biggest, smallest, roughest, smoothest, prettiest, etc., of the collec-

tion. Invite children to make signs and pictures explaining each item in their "museum." Some children might like to be "tour guides" for parents and others who want to view the collection.

Remember

▪ Some fives will want to build sculptures with rocks. Provide space in the art area for children to create with their favorite rocks. Those who want to save their creations can glue the rocks in place.
▪ Some fives will want to keep the rocks they find. Collect extras yourself so there will be plenty of rocks for everyone to study.

BOOKS

Place these books as resources in your science area during the rock study.	▪ *My Backyard* by Anne Rockwell (Macmillan)	▪ *Rock Collecting* by Roma Gans (Harper & Row)	▪ *Rocks and Minerals* by Alice Fitch-Martin and Bertha Morris-Parker (Golden Press "Exploring Earth Book")

ACTIVITY PLAN
READY-TO-USE TEACHING IDEAS FOR FIVES

SCIENCE

Try these icy explorations with your fives.

EXPERIMENTING WITH ICE

Aim: Children will observe, predict, and experiment to discover properties of ice.
Group size: Three or four children.
Materials: A metal cookie pan, a magnifying glass, ice-cube trays, three plastic bowls, and ice cubes.
In Advance: Arrange for access to a freezer.

GETTING READY

Use these activities to extend an experience that makes children curious about ice or about places where it's very cold. Invite them to name places where they have seen ice, both indoors (freezers, ice cube trays) and outdoors (icicles, skating rinks). Ask what children think ice is made of and how it's made. Provide lots of time for sharing ideas.

BEGIN

Show children the cookie pan. Ask, "What will happen if we put a little water on this pan and put it in the freezer?" Allow plenty of time for sharing ideas.

Dampen the pan and place it in a freezer overnight. Show children the ice crystals that have formed on it. Compare the results with their predictions of what would happen. Set out a magnifying glass for a close view of the crystals. Invite children to describe or draw pictures of what they see.

Now explore how and when ice melts. Number three bowls, then fill each with ice cubes. Invite children to predict what will happen if one bowl is placed in the freezer, one in the refrigerator, and one on the table. Record their predictions. Have children check the bowls every twenty minutes. Listen as they make comparisons and describe the changes in the ice. Check the predictions.

More Fun With Ice!

Icebergs in the Water Table — Give water play an arctic dimension! Freeze water in plastic containers, then add these "icebergs" to the water table. What happens to the temperature of the water as the ice melts? Or make colored ice cubes to add to the water table. Observe children's reactions as the ice melts.

Icebergs in the Desert? — Place a block of ice in the sand table. Observe children as they work with and around the ice. Ask them to describe how the sand changes as the ice melts.

If you try both iceberg tests, ask children where they think the ice melted faster — in the sand or the water. Encourage them to share their reasoning.

Build an Ice House — If you live in a cold climate, fill paper cartons with water and freeze overnight. Rip off the paper for ice blocks to build with outdoors. Be sure builders wear waterproof mittens.

Remember

▪ It's not unusual for fives to think that "Jack Frost" makes ice, so don't expect scientific answers to all your questions. Observation and hands-on experiences will help children recognize in time that it must be very cold for ice to form and stay solid.

BOOKS

Extend the focus on cold with these storytime books.

▪ *Katy and the Big Snow* by Virginia Burton (Houghton Mifflin)

▪ *The Snowy Day* by Ezra Jack Keats (Viking Penguin)

▪ *When Will It Snow?* by Syd Hoff (Harper & Row)

SCIENCE

Science can be a "dirty" business, but that's half the fun for fives.

WAKE UP, EARTH!

Aim: Children will observe, classify, and compare different types of soil.

Group size: Five or six children.

Materials: Small shovels or trowels, plastic bags, paper plates, magnifying glasses, a sieve or colander, a large plastic or glass container (or an aquarium), a watering can, plastic wrap, chart paper, and a marker.

GETTING READY

This is a good springtime activity, when children rediscover ground that was covered by snow and enjoy digging in moist soil. Ask, "Do you think all dirt is alike?" Give children plenty of time to share their ideas. Then invite them to try some experiments to test their ideas.

BEGIN

During playground time, have small groups of children take turns collecting samples of soil. Have each group take soil from at least two or three different places around the playground or school yard. Place dirt in plastic bags and label each sample.

Now set up a dirt discovery minicenter in your science area. Gather a magnifying glass, plates or pans for sorting, and a sieve for separating pebbles from the dirt samples. Add the soil samples.

Invite small groups to be "dirt detectives" by examining and comparing the different soil samples. Show children the different tools they have to work with, then stand back. Observe to see what interests children about the soil, such as the different colors, smells, and textures, and what discoveries they make about the composition of each. Record children's observations and discoveries. Repeat your original question: "Is all dirt alike?" See what kinds of responses you get now.

Bring Some Spring Inside

While on the playground, have the children help you dig a clump of ground (at least a six-inch cube) to study. Go deep enough to get a few layers of soil. Place the earth right side up, in one piece, inside a container such as an old aquarium.

Back in the room, have children observe the soil cube and describe what they see. What color is the dirt? Are there any worms or insects in it? Write their comments on an experience chart and date it.

Water the soil, cover it with plastic wrap, and place it near a sunny window. Encourage children to observe the changes they see and record each new set of observations on dated charts. As new plants and creatures appear, what may have seemed like "plain old ground" will suddenly come to life!

Remember

▪ After the children have observed the growth of the soil cube for a few weeks, if possible return it to the spot where it came from. This is modeling care and respect for the earth. Encourage children to compare how their soil looks to that around it.

▪ Be sure children always wash their hands after all digging and examining activities with soil.

BOOKS

Share these books that focus on facts about the earth.

▪ *About Garbage and Stuff* by Ann Z. Shanks (Viking)

▪ *The Little Park* by Dale Fife (Albert Whitman)

▪ *Wilson's World* by Edith Hurd (Harper & Row)

SCIENCE

Here's an exciting way to learn about shadows.

MAKE A SHADOW CLOCK

Aim: Children will observe, predict, and experiment as they investigate shadows.
Group size: Whole group.
Materials: Coffee can, dirt or sand, 2-foot stick or dowel, 12 stones, chalk, tempera paints, and a paintbrush.

GETTING READY

Invite children to look for shadows around the room. When they find shadows, ask them to guess what objects are making the shadows. How can they tell? Then suggest that children experiment by making their own hand shadows in a sunny spot in the room. Ask, "How do you make a shadow? What happens to the sunlight when a shadow is made?" Encourage children to continue to experiment so they begin to understand that shadows are formed when the light is blocked.

Next, help children see how shadows move throughout the day. Hang a simple shape in a sunny window so that its shadow makes a clear silhouette on the floor. First thing in the morning, gather together and use chalk to outline the shape's shadow. An hour later, check to see where the shadow shape is on the floor and mark its new position. Continue marking the shadow as it changes position throughout the day.

BEGIN

Explain to children that long ago people told time by using the shadows made by the sun because they knew that a shadow moves to a new position over the course of a day. Explain that today you are going to experiment with building your own shadow clock and watch as the shadow moves every hour. (This activity can be done outdoors or indoors near a sunny window.)

To construct the clock, ask children to fill the coffee can with moist sand or dirt, then press a stick into the center of the can so that the stick stands firmly in place. Move the can to a sunny area of the playground or by a sunny window. Place a small stone at the top of the shadow made by the stick. If it's about 9:00 a.m., help children paint a nine or make nine marks on the stone.

One hour later, check to see where the shadow of the stick appears and mark it with a new stone. Add the new numeral or number of marks to represent the new time. Repeat this process every hour to create a shadow clock for the hours of your school day. The next day, check to see if the clock is still accurate.

Remember

▪ At this age, it's not important for children to understand the process of rotation of the sun or its relationship to the formation of different shadow positions. The purpose of this activity is to give children experiences with the movement of shadows and opportunities to observe these changes.
▪ Encourage children to make shadow clocks at home where they can observe shadow movements for a longer period. (Send this plan home for families to try.)
▪ Some children will grasp the connection between the shadow clock and a real clock, but others won't. It's more important for children to see the regularity of a shadow's movements than to "tell time" with the clock.

BOOKS

Share these books about shadows with fives.

▪ *Come Out Shadows, Wherever You Are* by Bernice Myers (Scholastic)

▪ *The Owl Who Was Afraid of the Dark* by Jill Tomlinson (Viking)

▪ *Play With the Sun* by Howard E. Smith (McGraw-Hill)

SCIENCE

Fives will be amazed at what they learn about animals just by watching them.

ANIMAL OBSERVATIONS

Aim: Children will use observation and language skills as they learn about animals.

Group size: Four to six children, or whole group.

Materials: White drawing paper, crayons, and heavy cardboard or other hard surface to draw on outdoors; and colored construction paper and a stapler for constructing "field books."

In Advance: Scout around your playground or a nearby park for animals or insects children may see. Plan this activity for one of these areas. Look for nests on the ground that children might disturb. You want to observe but not disrupt animal life.

GETTING READY

Prepare children for a walk outside on your playground or in a nearby park to observe animals and insects. Invite them to be "naturalists." You might explain the term this way: "Naturalists are people who study animals. They go on investigations to see what an animal looks like and to watch how it moves, what it eats, and where it lives. Today we are all going to be naturalists as we follow animals outside on the playground (or in the park)."

BEGIN

Remind children to be *very* quiet when you first go outside so they don't frighten away animals that are nearby. Invite children to look carefully for animals or signs of animals. Encourage them to get down on the ground to look for insects or toads. Invite each child to observe one creature for a while. Remind them to stay in the playground or park. If their animal leaves the area, they can look for another to follow.

Bugs are an especially good choice because they move slowly and are easy to watch. Birds and squirrels are harder to keep up with and more easily frightened. Encourage children to quietly imitate the animals' movements as they observe. Later, when the group gathers to share their observations, invite children to take turns demonstrating how their animal moves.

A Field Book of Animal Observations

On the next walk, give children paper, crayons, and a hard surface to draw on. This time ask children to draw a picture of the animal or insect they observe. (Reassure children who think they can't draw the animal exactly that it's okay to draw it in their own way.) Have children sign and date their drawings. Invite them to dictate something they noticed about the animal on a separate sheet of paper. Collate the drawings and observations into a group field guide.

Remember

- This is a wonderful activity to do once a week over a period of time so that children get to see how different animals' activities change with the seasons.
- Fives are old enough to start using children's resource materials to "research" information. Plan a trip to a library to look for books about animals.
- Children can also learn a lot from observing such creatures as hamsters, guinea pigs, and goldfish in the room. Add entries on these animals to the guide.

BOOKS

Here are some animal books to share at storytime.

- *A Year of Birds* by Ashley Wolff (Dodd, Mead)

- *Frederick* by Leo Lionni (Random House)

- *The Goodnight Circle* by Carolyn Lesser (Harcourt Brace Jovanovich)

SCIENCE

This problem-solving activity will get fives thinking about simple tools they see.

WHAT CAN YOU USE TO BEAT AN EGG?

Aim: Children will use observation, prediction, problem-solving, and language skills as they experiment with different ways to mix eggs.

Group size: Four or five children.

Materials: Raw eggs; small mixing bowls; any or all of the following: fork, wire whisk, rotary egg beater, small jar with a tight-fitting lid, potato masher, vegetable steamer, and measuring spoons; electric frying pan; oil or margarine; wooden spoon; paper plates; plastic spoons; napkins; and chart paper and a marker.

GETTING READY

Start the activity with a discussion about scrambled eggs. Ask, "Do you ever eat scrambled eggs? How do the eggs get scrambled? How does the inside of an egg look when you crack the shell?" Give children ample time to share ideas. Make a list on chart paper of the different ways they think eggs get scrambled.

BEGIN

Display a variety of cooking tools for children to examine and discuss. Try to include some that are not commonly used to beat eggs, like measuring spoons, a potato masher, or a vegetable steamer.

When children have had ample time to review the tools, ask, "Which tools do you think we can use to beat the eggs? Which ones do you think will do the best job?" Have children place the tools in order from "best" to "worst." Tape a number on each tool to remember its place in line.

Using one egg at a time, have children try out the fork, whisk, rotary egg beater, etc. (Many children particularly enjoy shaking an egg in a jar and are often surprised by the results.) Ask children to observe the texture of each egg. Invite them to decide on characteristics that show the egg is well mixed, such as foamy texture, no yolk showing, etc.

When all the tools have been tested, have children reorder them based on the results of their experiments. The numbers provide a way to check their earlier predictions.

After all the fun, don't forget to cook the eggs! Discuss the experience as children enjoy this snack.

Remember

▪ Fives are much more "scientific" than threes or fours. They are fascinated by this type of analysis. It's best to avoid directing this activity too much so that their natural inquisitiveness comes out.

Let them do the talking and problem-solving, but be there quietly, ready to facilitate with a question when needed. Of course, take over as chef when it's time to cook the now-beaten eggs!

▪ Be sure the dramatic-play corner has plenty of household tools so that children can continue experimenting during this kind of play.

▪ If you don't want to make scrambled eggs, this activity works just as well with powdered or liquid soap. Focus on which tool makes the best bubbles.

BOOKS

Share these books at storytime to add to the fun.	▪ *Green Eggs and Ham* by Dr. Seuss (Random House)	▪ *Pancakes, Pancakes* by Eric Carle (Alfred A. Knopf)	▪ *Scrambled Eggs Super!* by Dr. Seuss (Random House)

ACTIVITY PLAN INDEX:
TWOS AND THREES

DEVELOPMENTAL AREAS AND SKILLS ENHANCED	PROCESS SKILLS						DEVELOPMENTAL SKILLS					
	Observing	Classifying	Quantifying	Predicting	Experimenting	Communicating	Creative Expression	Social Interaction	Cooperation/Sharing	Problem Solving	Expressing Emotions	Fine Motor
2'S ACTIVITY PLANS												
FUN WITH FLASHLIGHTS PAGE 38	■				■	■		■			■	■
RAIN AND SNOW ADVENTURES PAGE 39	■				■	■					■	■
FUN WITH BALLS AND TUBES PAGE 40	■				■	■		■		■		■
INDOOR/OUTDOOR FEELY FUN! PAGE 41	■	■			■	■					■	■
JOIN THE TASTING PARTY! PAGE 42	■	■				■		■				■
WATCH THE WIND PAGE 43	■			■	■						■	■
FOR THE BIRDS PAGE 44	■					■		■			■	■
HOLDING THEIR OWN PAGE 45	■	■		■	■							■
MAGNIFICENT MAGNETS PAGE 46	■	■		■	■							■
LET'S GROW GRASS PAGE 47	■					■						■
3'S ACTIVITY PLANS												
CREATE A TEXTURE BOOK PAGE 48	■	■			■	■	■	■			■	■
A NOSE WORKOUT PAGE 49	■				■	■	■		■		■	■
TAKE A NATURE WALK PAGE 50	■	■		■	■	■		■			■	■
WHAT MAKES THE BEST BUBBLES? PAGE 51	■		■		■	■		■		■	■	■
EXPERIMENTING WITH WET AND DRY PAGE 52	■			■	■	■		■		■		
HAVE A MUD DAY! PAGE 53	■			■	■	■		■		■	■	■
SHADOW HUNTING PAGE 54	■		■		■	■		■				■
MIRROR, MIRROR, ON THE WALL ... PAGE 55	■				■	■		■	■			
A PICNIC FOR ANTS PAGE 56	■			■		■		■			■	■
HOW CAN WE MOVE THIS BOX OF BLOCKS? PAGE 57	■				■	■				■	■	■

ACTIVITY PLAN INDEX:
FOURS AND FIVES

DEVELOPMENTAL AREAS AND SKILLS ENHANCED	Observing	Classifying	Quantifying	Predicting	Experimenting	Communicating	Creative Expression	Social Interaction	Cooperation/ Sharing	Problem Solving	Expressing Emotions	Fine Motor
4'S ACTIVITY PLANS												
JOIN IN AN OBSERVATION GAME! PAGE 58	■					■	■	■		■		
PREDICTING WITH CONTAINERS AND SAND PAGE 59	■		■	■	■	■				■	■	
WHERE DOES THE WATER GO? PAGE 60	■		■	■	■	■				■	■	■
FUN WITH MAGNETS PAGE 61	■	■		■	■	■		■			■	
TAKING THE HEAT PAGE 62	■			■	■	■			■	■		■
BE WIND DETECTIVES! PAGE 63	■				■	■		■		■	■	
PLANTING TERRARIUMS PAGE 64	■			■	■	■			■		■	
BUILD A WORM FARM PAGE 65	■			■		■			■	■	■	
ADOPT A WEED PAGE 66	■		■	■		■	■			■	■	■
WHAT'S INSIDE OF ME? PAGE 67	■				■	■		■		■		
5'S ACTIVITY PLANS												
LET IT RAIN! PAGE 68	■		■	■	■	■			■	■	■	
EXPERIMENTING WITH TEMPERATURE PAGE 69	■		■	■	■				■	■		■
PLANTING BULBS PAGE 70	■	■	■			■				■		■
SANDBOX SCIENTISTS PAGE 71	■	■				■	■	■	■	■	■	
BE "ROCK HOUNDS" PAGE 72	■	■	■	■	■	■	■	■	■	■	■	■
EXPERIMENTING WITH ICE PAGE 73	■			■	■	■			■	■	■	■
WAKE UP, EARTH! PAGE 74	■	■		■	■	■			■		■	
MAKE A SHADOW CLOCK PAGE 75	■		■	■	■	■			■		■	
ANIMAL OBSERVATIONS PAGE 76	■					■	■		■	■	■	■
WHAT CAN YOU USE TO BEAT AN EGG? PAGE 77	■	■		■	■				■	■	■	

RESOURCES

These materials can help you gain a better understanding of how to plan for and encourage science exploration and discovery in your early childhood program. Look for these books, articles, and magazines in bookstores and libraries.

ACTIVITY BOOKS

▼ *Bubbles, Rainbows, and Worms* by Sam Ed Brown (Gryphon House)

▼ *Hug a Tree and Other Things to Do Outdoors* by Robert E. Rockwell, Elizabeth A. Sherwood, and Robert A. Williams (Gryphon House)

▼ *Let's Play Science* by Mary Stetton-Carson (Harper & Row)

▼ *Mudpies to Magnets: A Preschool Science Curriculum* by Robert A. Williams, Robert E. Rockwell, and Elizabeth A. Sherwood (Gryphon House)

▼ *Open the Door, Let's Explore: Neighborhood Field Trips for Young Children* by Rhoda Redleaf (Toys-n-Things Press)

▼ *Science with Young Children* by Bess-Gene Holt (NAEYC)

▼ *What Will Happen If ... : Young Children and the Scientific Method* by Barbara Sprung, Merle Froschl, Patricia B. Campbell (Educational Equity Concepts)

ARTICLES

▼ "Learning Mathematics and Science Through Play" by Michael Henniger, *Journal of Research in Childhood Education*, February 1987

▼ "Science and the Early Childhood Curriculum: One Thing Leads to Another" by Maryann Ziemer, *Young Children*, September 1987

▼ "Setting the Stage for Science Discoveries" by Bess-Gene Holt, Scholastic *Pre-K Today*, February 1990

▼ "Wonderscience!" by Wendy Nichols and Kim Nichols, Scholastic *Pre-K Today*, May/June 1991

▼ "The World at Their Fingertips: Children in Museums" by Mary K. Judd and James B. Kracht, *Learning Opportunities Beyond the School*, 1987, published by Association for Childhood Education International

MATERIALS

The groups below offer various games, posters, children's magazines, and other kinds of materials to support science explorations. Write for catalogs or information at the addresses below. Unless noted, materials are free.

▼ Dover Nature Books Catalog, Dover Publications, 31 East 2nd St., Mineola, NY 11501

▼ National Arbor Day Foundation, 100 Arbor Ave., Nebraska City, NE 68410 (ask about membership information)

▼ National Geographic Society Catalog, P.O. Box 2118, Washington, DC 20013

▼ National Wildlife Federation Catalog, Membership Services, 8925 Leefberg Pike, Vienna, VA 22184-0001; (They publish *Your Big Backyard* magazine for ages 3-5.)

▼ *Owl* and *Chickadee* magazines, Subscription Department, 56 The Espalande, Suite 304, Toronto M5E 1A7, Canada; (Subscriptions are $3.50.)

▼ Zoobooks, 3590 Kettner Blvd., San Diego, CA 92101